BRINGING IT HOME®

ENGLAND

BRINGING IT HOME®
ENGLAND

THE ULTIMATE GUIDE TO CREATING THE FEELING OF ENGLAND IN YOUR HOME

CHERYL MACLACHLAN

WITH BO NILES

PHOTOGRAPHS BY
IVAN TERESTCHENKO

FROM THE BRINGING IT HOME® SERIES

CLARKSON POTTER/PUBLISHERS
NEW YORK

To Fred,

THE STAR BY WHICH

I CHART ALL MY JOURNEYS.

Love, Cheryl

COPYRIGHT © 1998 BY CHERYL MacLACHLAN
ILLUSTRATIONS COPYRIGHT © 1998 BY IVAN TERESTCHENKO

PUBLISHED BY CLARKSON N. POTTER/PUBLISHERS, 201 EAST 50TH STREET,
NEW YORK, NEW YORK 10022. MEMBER OF THE CROWN PUBLISHING GROUP.

RANDOM HOUSE, INC. NEW YORK, TORONTO, LONDON, SYDNEY, AUCKLAND
WWW.RANDOMHOUSE.COM

CLARKSON N. POTTER, POTTER,
AND COLOPHON ARE TRADEMARKS OF CLARKSON N. POTTER, INC.

PRINTED IN CHINA

DESIGN BY DONNA AGAJANIAN AND LISA SLOANE

LIBRARY OF CONGRESS CATALOGING-IN-PUBLICATION DATA
MacLACHLAN, CHERYL.
BRINGING IT HOME—ENGLAND : CHERYL MacLACHLAN ; PHOTOGRAPHS BY IVAN
TERESTCHENKO. — 1ST ED.
INCLUDES INDEX.
1. INTERIOR DECORATION—ENGLISH INFLUENCES. 2. HOUSE FURNISHINGS—
ENGLAND. I. TITLE.
TX311.M2353 1998
645—DC21   97-35941

ISBN 0-517-70782-9

10 9 8 7 6 5 4 3

ACKNOWLEDGMENTS

Working in another country—even when one speaks the language—can be a daunting task. Deadlines loom large, rain arrives at inopportune moments, and steering wheels appear with alarming regularity in front of passenger seats. In England, however, these concerns proved trifling. The bountiful enthusiasm, gracious hospitality, and extraordinary wit of the English people allowed even the most challenging shoots to flow smoothly and the tightest of schedules to mesh seamlessly. I owe a debt of gratitude (not to mention a vastly enriched vocabulary) to many who opened their homes and shared their best stories. In particular I would like to thank:

Polly Devlin, Andy Garnet, and their daughters Rose, Daisy, and Bay, who warmly welcomed Ivan and me to their beautiful home and dazzled us with insight into the English psyche both humorous and piercing. Sue Young, a Londoner who moved to Paris and opened a cooking school—and is thus the most courageous woman I know—for pointing me in all the right directions. Alison and Jeremy Gibbs, whose knowledge and talent in the garden is so exquisitely complemented by their personal grace and charm. And Ali Edney, who gave so freely of her time and talent and whose beautiful spirit left a wonderful impression on Ivan and me.

And to all of the following people who helped in so many ways, I wish space permitted me to address you all individually. My warmest appreciation to:

Alidad	Meredith Harrington	Jane Levitz
Kate, Ned, Lilly, Tom, and Jack Barton	Ninette Hewitt and	Gordon Lindsay
Diane Berger	Michael Thornton	Ann-Louise Little
Elizabeth Blaker	Virginia Howard	Mair Lloyd
Nina Campbell	Sue and John Hume	Maxime and Bill Magan
George Cooper	Helen and Andrew Kilpatrick	Becky Metcalfe
Christine, Charlotte, and Harry Elliott	Maddy, Emily, and Katie Kingzett	Sally Metcalfe
Anne, Duncan, and Victoria Goodhew	Henrietta Konig	Jacqui Moore
Sarah Gough	Kelly Kurz	Peggy Post
Anne Hardy	Marsha Lasky	Nicholas and Vera Wright

And finally, I want to thank the team who helped to create *Bringing It Home—England:* Ivan Terestchenko, the genius behind all the photography, illustrations, and watercolors in this book; Annetta Hanna, my wonderful and talented editor; Bo Niles, whose expertise in architecture and the decorative arts brought greater depth and precision to my manuscript; Jane Treuhaft, Clarkson Potter's Associate Art Director, who from the first book has devoted untold hours to shaping the elegant design of this series; Lisa Sloane, who joins the team with this book, for all her beautiful work on the layout; and to the guiding lights of Clarkson Potter—Art Director Marysarah Quinn, Editorial Director Lauren Shakely, and Crown President Chip Gibson—for their continued support. Also at Clarkson Potter and Crown my warmest appreciation to the doyennes of public relations Wendy Schuman and Mary Ellen Briggs and to John Son for being so helpful at every stage of this book. And, in the category of last but most certainly not least, my terrific agent Jeff Stone has my devotion for all his help and good advice.

CONTENTS

I INTRODUCTION

4 THE SUBSTANCE OF ENGLISH STYLE

The common threads that unite all English homes: a penchant for comfort; visually charged interiors; rich, dark-hued woods; bird and botanical motifs; strong graphics; and a devotion to nurturing the eccentric.

38 THE LIVING ROOM

Ideas for creating the look of a traditional English drawing room. How to arrange the furniture. What fabrics to select. Plus, a guide to the most important English architects and designers.

84 THE BEDROOM

A cozy sanctuary. How to create romantic walls and windows. Decorating the bath with an English touch, and a look at the magical atmosphere of the nursery.

114 The Dining Room

How to evoke the handsomely tailored look of a traditional English dining room.
Working with bold, daring colors. Learn more about fine English silver, porcelain,
and crystal. Plus, a guide to selecting tables and chairs.

140 The Garden

It is said that the garden is the English art form. Learn about creating structure,
designing proper beds and borders, framing a view, and using containers.
A look at conservatories and at the art of flower arranging.

152 The Kitchen

A big, cozy place filled with chunky pine furniture and a robust old-fashioned
"cooker." A look at unfitted cabinetry. What to do with the floors.
Plus, the pleasure of taking tea and an idea notebook.

177 Resources

Where to find all the essential materials for creating the feeling of England in
your home. Plus, travel ideas and a reading list.

182 Index

INTRODUCTION

Eight of us were gathered in front of a crackling fire in a richly appointed drawing room. Nestled into an assortment of club chairs, we sipped after-dinner drinks and entertained the relative merits of several parlor games. A consensus was achieved on "Book," a spirited game employing titles pulled at random from the library shelves. Using one book per round, a chairperson reads aloud the pithy synopsis found on its dust jacket. Armed with blank cards on which to record their entries, each player then invents a convincing final sentence for the tome. Meanwhile the chairperson (a revolving duty) writes the actual last sentence on a card. Entries are passed to the chairperson, shuffled to preserve anonymity, read aloud to the group, and then voted upon. Points are earned by correctly identifying the real last line — or by creating brilliant decoys that lure the votes of others.

Being a writer and possessing a firm command of the native tongue, I felt quite confident and indeed was scoring admirably in the early rounds. After a half hour of rousing fun, a slim little text was presented. Entitled *The Parish Churches of England*, it earnestly surveyed the spiritual and architectural treasures of the land. I emulated the book's sincere tone and submitted what I believed to be a winning entry: "Thus we can see that whether late Norman or early Gothic, high-towered Perpendicular or simple Modern, the true role of the parish church is, after all, to shelter the soul."

Anticipating a neat booty of votes, I was instead met by peals of laughter. Withering in the kind of embarrassment that can arise only from misguided arrogance, I heard a hearty voice cry: "Oh, jolly good effort! But it is so obviously Cheryl's because the poor little American doesn't realize there is no such thing as a Modern parish church."

They were right. Surrounded by the seeming trappings of my own Anglo-Saxon culture, I forgot how distinct — and therefore intriguing — England is. I grew up in Massachusetts (where, by the way, Modern parish churches coexist with the storybook white clapboard types) amid prep schools, lawn clubs, and towns named for the English places from whence the colonists had come. After completing books on France, Italy, and Sweden — cultures exotically different from my own — I imagined that in writing this volume of Bringing It Home® I would indulge in the pleasure of "going home," so to speak.

What I experienced was a feeling much more exhilarating. It was a double joy of going to a foreign land where the initial adjustment is quite easy, but where beyond the obvious similarities lies an endless stream of discovery. Even when viewed through the prism of traditional style and culture, America and England are deliciously different. In *Bringing It Home®—England* I have tried to share the richness of looking more deeply into the things I thought I already knew. I hope my journey proves as inspiring to you as it did to me.

HOW TO USE THIS BOOK

The more I learn about the decorative arts, the more I understand why it is so hard to say definitively what is an English style, a French style, and so forth. History gets in the way. For centuries, ruling families throughout Europe often intermarried as a means of consolidating power or ensuring peace. Naturally, customs and aesthetic preferences would travel with the betrothed. It was also commonplace for a monarch to seek out the decorative riches of a neighbor: Russia's Catherine the Great brought English treasures to the Hermitage. England's George IV adored French designs, furnishing his residence, Carlton House, with countless pieces from Paris. And there were the decorative repercussions of archaeological work: the excavations of Pompeii inspired the designs of England's Robert Adam as well as the Court Style of France's Louis XVI and Sweden's Gustav III.

With so much intermingling of the cultures, one might wonder if such a thing as a national style could truly exist. Yet cultures do in fact have their own distinct styles. The endlessly intersecting currents of design have simply culminated in a rich and expansive menu from which each country orders à la carte. Thus, "English style" refers to the unique constellation of elements—homegrown and foreign—that the English have taken as their own. A dining room, for example, might include blue-and-white porcelain inspired by the Orient, brightly colored chintz borrowed from India, Honduran mahogany made up into a Georgian-style dining table, and a richly patterned Persian carpet. Any one of these items, used in its native land, would be disposed quite differently.

Bringing It Home®—England focuses on the aesthetic preferences that form the foundations of English style, such as the love of rich, dark woods, or the affinity for graphically strong motifs. I have purposefully emphasized traditional styles because contemporary trends are sometimes "temporary" trends, and may not be widely accepted in the long run.

Like a house, *Bringing It Home®—England* is divided into rooms. After a brief overview of the common threads running throughout an English home, we look at the characteristics of each room, beginning with the living room. Where such aspects overlap—in the way a window is dressed, for example—the subject is treated only once. An "Idea Notebook" at the conclusion of each chapter provides specific decorating suggestions for evoking an English atmosphere in your home. And finally, there are chapters on the beloved English traditions of gardening and hosting an afternoon tea.

Bringing It Home®—England is a guide to enriching your home the English way. Unlike a guide, however, it does not impose a rigid set of rules. Re-create whatever strikes your fancy. Pick and choose according to your own tastes and desires. After all, there is a reason why these are called the "decorative arts" and not the "decorative sciences."

OPPOSITE: Classic Laura Ashley cottons, featuring soft, rambling flowers, make for an idyllic corner in the sitting room of Llangoed Hall.

3

THE SUBSTANCE OF
ENGLISH
STYLE

English style fascinates the eye. Like the colorful dynasties that have comprised England's monarchy from the Normans to the House of Windsor, English style is kaleidoscopic in its complexity. It has evolved over the centuries, but has always resisted radical change. It has reached around the globe for inspiration, but has always remained fiercely loyal to its national character. It refuses to be absorbed in a single glance, but rather

Interior designer Sally Metcalfe created a room that is both elegant and comfortable by focusing on classically styled and beautifully upholstered furnishings.

demands to be explored as a series of intricately constructed vignettes.

Distilled to the overarching qualities that have endured since the reign of Elizabeth I, English style can be described as an engaging tapestry weaving together the following attributes: a penchant for comfort, an inclination toward visually charged interiors, a preference for rich, dark-hued woods, a fondness for bird and botanical motifs, an affinity for strong graphics, and a devotion to nurturing the idiosyncratic and the eccentric.

A PENCHANT FOR
COMFORT

Two adjectives often applied to English houses, particularly to the so-called English country house, are "cozy" and "welcoming." In no small measure, these perceptions are linked to the British preoccupation with comfort. Houses are generously "upholstered"; they abound with overstuffed sofas and chairs, throw pillows of every size and shape, cushioned window seats, and breakfast nooks—all accented with snuggly woolen shawls to toss over one's shoulders at the first sign of a chill. Even dogs, of which the British are extremely fond, enjoy amply padded wicker baskets. While a stiff upper lip may be required in society, at home the emphasis is decidedly on comfort.

Using ample groupings of throw pillows, such as these from Liberty, creates a cozy English feeling in any room.

LEFT AND BELOW: The majority of English upholstered furniture features loose cushions filled with a combination of down, feathers, and sometimes other fillers. The exceptional lofting power of the down creates the quintessentially English "overstuffed" style.

CONSIDER COMBINING COMFORT WITH PRACTICALITY. MANY HOMES HAVE SMALL NOOKS, BAY WINDOWS, OR UNUSED CORNERS THAT CAN BE CONVERTED INTO COZY RETREATS. BUILD A WOODEN PLATFORM INTO THE SPACE TO HOUSE DRAWERS OR CABINETS. TOP IT WITH A CUSHION AND FINISH WITH A GENEROUS SUPPLY OF THROW PILLOWS.

To create this feeling of ease in your interior, focus on the myriad details that might make a room warm and inviting. Pile extra pillows on sofas, chairs, and beds—especially where family members tend to congregate. Select ample, even oversized, seating. Pad surfaces wherever possible; for example, let a tufted upholstered bench stand in for a coffee table, or draw up a cushioned footstool near a reading chair. Don't skimp on the textiles. Layer a kilim rug or two on top of rush or sisal matting for extra softness underfoot. Drape windows rather than using blinds or shutters. Upholster walls. Pleat lampshades to soften any light that might appear glaring and harsh to the eye.

Comfort also translates into the small touches that make daily life just a bit more pleasant for family members and guests alike. A much discussed book or an unusual periodical is never more than an arm's length away from a cozy reading seat. Nosegays of fresh flowers brighten spots where people are apt to gather. A guest room might be equipped with an electric teakettle set upon a tray with a pretty porcelain tea service, a delicious array of teas, and a tin of biscuits.

The variations on the theme of comfort are endless, but the underlying principle never wavers: home is a sanctuary and life inside its walls should always be as agreeable as possible.

BELOW: Never hesitate to put several large-scale pieces together in one room. The resulting feeling will be warm and intimate. RIGHT: Mixing several fabric motifs in a small nook can make the space feel cozy.

A VISUALLY CHARGED ATMOSPHERE

A witty observer of her fellow country-men, London-based novelist Polly Devlin offers a description for the visually charged atmosphere that pervades the vast majority of English homes: "It looks as if the family has picked up every last stick of furniture from the ancestral seat and squeezed it into a dwelling of manageable proportions," she laughs. Many English, in other words, shoehorn an abundance of diverse furnishings into every conceivable nook and cranny.

English interiors are marvelously rich, embracing a tremendous range and complexity of patterns and colors. A luxuriant overlapping of textiles—carpets, upholstery, drapery, and wall coverings—is fundamental to re-creating this feeling. Striking motifs, be they botanical, heraldic, or geometric, dominate. And although one single pattern may be repeated—on a pair of armchairs, or at a window and upon a bed, for example—the overall character of a room is rooted in the adventurous syncopation and juxtaposition of many motifs. The English, in a word, rarely select a solid textile when a pattern is available.

Furnishings, often a mixture of fine

In her London library, Sally Metcalfe creates a rich and welcoming visual texture by combining materials as varied as bamboo and marble and creating capacious bookshelves to house her favorite titles.

LEFT: Designer Christophe Gollut creates visual drama through the use of deep, rich colors and bold patterns. ABOVE: London-based designer Alidad's brilliant combination of patterns extends even to the ceiling. Here he used a sumptuous paper of his own design.

DON'T HESITATE TO PLACE PERSIAN RUGS OF VARIED MOTIFS IN THE SAME ROOM. A LARGE SPACE CAN EASILY ACCOMMODATE TWO OR THREE RUGS. THEY WILL HELP TO DEFINE INDIVIDUAL SEATING AREAS, AND THE VARIETY OF PATTERNS AND COLORS WILL ADD VISUAL RICHNESS TO THE DECOR.

heirlooms and flea market treasures, come from many different epochs and inhabit every available inch of space. (Only in museums does one see a room decorated in a "pure" period style.) Resting upon a panoply of tabletops, mantelpieces, and shelves is a vast array of collectibles: Staffordshire dogs, silver and brass candlesticks, framed photographs—the possibilities are infinite. To the untrained eye, these objects might appear as unruly clutter. On the contrary, however, collections are arranged with clear intent and purpose. "You must always keep your clutter well organized," counsels one thoughtful homemaker, "or it will soon turn into a muddle."

The walls of the rooms are an important element in creating the visually charged atmosphere characteristic of the English style. Consider your color scheme with care. Although such schemes have evolved over the centuries—from daring Regency combinations such as emerald and crimson to subtle Adamesque robin's-egg blue and pearl gray, for example— English color palettes (and the motifs in which they are rendered) contribute an undeniable energy to a room. Adding further visual interest is the manner in which art is displayed upon the wall, a subject we will consider in the next chapter.

ABOVE: The display of collections is an effective way to bring visual texture into a room. RIGHT: Peggy Post has re-created a delightful echo of Bloomsbury in her London kitchen.

RICH, DARK
WOODS

Imagine the scene: a fine port is cradled in a crystal decanter, a curl of smoke rises from a pipe, a copy of the London *Times* lies folded on a brilliantly polished mahogany table. Now, replace the mahogany with beech or ash. Not only does the image crumble, but one quickly realizes the importance of dark woods to the traditional English aesthetic.

Even the most cursory examination of the history of English furniture reveals the country's romance with rich, deep-hued woods. From the outset and particularly during the Queen Anne (1702–1714) and early Georgian periods (1714–1760), walnut was the favorite choice of monarchs and cabinetmakers alike. Later in the century, when disease struck the walnut trees in France, exterminating England's principal resource for the wood, the British turned to mahogany from the Caribbean and Central America, with which they regularly traded. Mahogany, with its even, close grain and magnificent warm tones, quickly became the new darling of the decorating classes. In fact, the most renowned names in the English decorative arts—Robert Adam, Thomas Chippendale, and Thomas Sheraton—enthusiastically endorsed mahog-

Richly hued woods such as mahogany and walnut are essential to capturing the traditional English aesthetic. Think of ways to weave them into your decor not only with furniture, but also through custom paneling, stairways, and other built-in features.

To enhance the presence of dark woods in your interior, consider the many nonfurniture items that can be crafted in oak, mahogany, walnut, and other deep-hued woods. Frames for mirrors and paintings, decorative boxes, and lamps are but a few examples. Additionally, architectural elements such as wainscoting and moldings, rendered in dark woods, will evoke an English style.

Right: A magnificent Jacobean dining table and chairs rendered in walnut impart a rich and stately tone to this room. Opposite: Natural light falling across raised-panel shutters enhances their beauty.

any as the most suitable wood for creating the "proper" look, particularly with regard to the dining room. The opinions of these designers clearly made an indelible impact: today we continue to regard mahogany as the quintessential wood of the late Georgian or Regency period, and mahogany is still considered the most elegant wood for traditional dining room furniture.

From 1601, when Elizabeth I granted the East India Company an exclusive charter to trade in the Far East, the Orient also proved an important influence on the English love of deep, rich wood tones. While not constructed of a dark wood per se, furniture lacquered in a manner known as "japanning" or "chinoiserie" is revered by the English. In a related spirit, paints and stains have often been employed to enhance woods of a lesser quality. Graining in the fashion of

mahogany, for example, is a practice that has long been condoned.

Alongside this rich spectrum of dark woods, two pale, warm-toned exceptions cannot be overlooked. Light satinwoods were favored by the neoclassicist designers and cabinetmakers of the late Georgian period. And, in recent decades, scrubbed pine fashioned into dressers, sideboards, and plateracks has become practically synonymous with the English country kitchen style. (Pushing the "light" decorative envelope was the stylist Syrie Maugham, who created a stir, if not a scandal, when she confected the all-white room.)

While pine is an excellent choice for a kitchen, a traditional English look throughout the rest of the house will be more effectively achieved by selecting dark woods for the majority of your furnishings.

A Celebration of **Flora** and **Fauna**

If Faunas, the Roman god of animals, and Flora, the goddess of flowers, were still with us, they would be tickled pink by the way things have turned out in England. Not only do the British devote themselves body and soul to the art of gardening, they also revere all creatures great and small. Indeed, a wide variety of philanthropic organizations dedicated to animals have been founded in England, ranging from the globally famous World Wildlife Fund to the decidedly more low-key Hospital for Hedgehogs.

Inside the home, the celebration of flora is reflected in the spectacular array of flowers and foliage that adorn everything from draperies to dinnerware. When asked to consider fabrics, for example, we may reflexively think of the chintzes for which England is legendary, but magnificent flowers and plants are also woven into tapestries, rendered in needlepoint, or embroidered on bedding or table linens. Wallpapers, carpets, and lampshades are also often imprinted with blossoms, leaves, and vines. Watercolor or oil paintings of the garden's treasures can be found displayed throughout the home.

When decorating your own home, take your cue from the cottage garden

Bennison's "Roses" is emblematic of the English genius for celebrating nature in the decorative arts.

Botanical motifs are woven into every aspect of the English decor. LEFT: Author Diane Berger selected a floral print for her kitchen. ABOVE: Designer George Cooper sets a collection of butterfly prints against a leaf-patterned wallpaper. RIGHT: Interior designer Ann-Louise Little chose a pretty yellow rose design for the wallpaper and headboard of her bedroom.

ENGLISH
STYLE

25

Rather than repre-
senting the forms of
nature in an abstract
or simplified manner,
the English take great
care to imbue natural
motifs with exquisite
detail, as can be seen
by the sampling of
objects on these
two pages.

bursting with many varieties of plants and flowers, and feel free to combine botanical motifs in your interior. Consider, for example, draping one chintz at the bedroom windows and another over your bed; add a chain-stitch rug with yet another floral motif, and finish with porcelain lamp bases painted with an Oriental floral pattern.

The animal kingdom, too, is richly represented in the decorative arts, particularly with regard to birds and dogs. When the American artist James McNeill Whistler was living in London, he created a sensation with his Peacock Room painted for the industrialist Frederick R. Leyland (now installed in the Freer Gallery in Washington, D.C.). William Morris used birds in many of his most beloved designs. Additionally, the British have long been influenced by Asian art, in which the bird, especially the crane, holds almost a sacred status.

Man's best friend is also represented copiously throughout the English home. Beautifully worked charcoal or oil portraits of the family dog, often commissioned from well-known artists, grace the walls of many an English home. The family pet is immortalized in needlepoints covering footstools and throw pillows. His likeness may show up in pottery, small silver trinkets, and, if the budget allows, maybe even in bronze!

LEFT: Channel grooves and other exquisite detailing bring an appealing graphic quality to this fireplace surround. RIGHT: Strict symmetry and crisp forms have been used to create a dramatic and handsome entry. BELOW: The English never hesitate to pair boldly contrasting colors, like the snowy white and inky black of this facade.

STRIKINGLY
GRAPHIC

The uniform of the beefeater, with its bright red jacket, starched white sashes, and towering black fur hat, serves to reinforce a simple truth about the English aesthetic: bold is best. A quick drive through London reveals an urban architecture that is crisp and graphic. Witness, for example, the juxtaposition of snowy-white facades and inky-black railings, an eye-catching cherry-red front door or Britain's trademark telephone booth. Unlike the soft colors and undulating curves that characterize Paris, the angles and colors of London are clean, bright, and sharp.

The love of strong graphics plays out in myriad ways. Stripes are a favorite pattern for wall coverings. Mahogany furniture etches a pronounced silhouette against its background. Paintings hung in dense groupings create an energizing visual statement. Fireplace surrounds often feature sharp rectangular forms chiseled with channel grooves. Colors are daring and unexpected. Even floral motifs are sometimes made more vibrant by outlining flowers and vines with a fine-tooled line.

In decorating your own home, do not shy away from strong contrasts or crisp geometric forms. With the exception of the "faded chintz" look (which creates a definite aesthetic in its own right), the impression of a home decorated in traditional English style is not soft and retiring but rather deliciously invigorating.

ABOVE: Stripes are a favorite wall pattern because they lend vibrancy to a room. LEFT: The placement of art in dense groupings is an effective way to create graphic interest in a room. RIGHT: Deeply hued wood contrasts beautifully with light-toned fabric.

A Tad
Eccentric

"There is only one thing in the world worse than being talked about, " wrote Oscar Wilde in *The Picture of Dorian Gray*, "and that is not being talked about." Perhaps this philosophy lies behind the unusual ability of the English to cultivate eccentricity in every aspect of their lives—and homes. Entire sections of a house may be given over to a family pet. Grown-ups may play in their own tree houses. Teddy bears may take a seat at the dinner table. (Speaking of teddy bears, who can forget the character of Sebastian in Evelyn Waugh's novel *Brideshead Revisited*, who contemplates a travel decision involving his own teddy bear, Aloyisius: "I have a good mind not to take Aloyisius to Venice. I don't want him to meet a lot of horrid Italian bears and pick up bad habits.") By definition the boundaries of eccentric behavior, and subsequently its manifestation in the decor of a house, are without limit.

Re-creating this aspect of English style in your own home is the decorating equivalent of dancing around a land mine. One cannot purposefully do something in

In the view of writer Polly Devlin one can never be too devoted to man's best friend. In her Somerset home she has devoted an entire room to canine art.

order to be "eccentric." Indeed, that sort of calculated behavior would clearly deserve the pejorative moniker "affected." True eccentricity works because it is, well, truly eccentric.

Perhaps the best advice in this area is to approach the problem from another perspective: Don't stop yourself from doing something outrageous, even if "proper society" might disapprove. Down deep, each of us has a passion or fantasy that we might never have been encouraged to pursue. If you've always harbored a love of gilded birdcages, go out and collect them with a vengeance. If you go weak at the knees over sundials, give yourself free rein. Over time, you'll revel in the evolution of a heretofore undeveloped part of your character—and your decor just may grow more interesting in the process!

Although her birth certificate would suggest otherwise, author Diane Berger fancies herself a woman of the eighteenth century, and has skillfully fashioned the proper setting in her London town house.

A sampling of eccentricity.
CLOCKWISE FROM TOP LEFT:
A "tree house"; this bear
guards a stairway; nattily
attired busts; an under-
cover bear; garden furni-
ture with a sense of humor;
portrait of a loved one;
dancing frogs; and an
Arabian dog tent.

SALLY DUCHESS

THE
LIVING
ROOM

The main public room in the English house is properly referred to as the "drawing room," not because its occupants devote their time to charcoal studies, but rather because it once was customary for women to "withdraw" to this room after dinner, leaving the dining room to their husbands and escorts, who preferred to take a cigar and port in fraternal privacy.

Today the drawing room has redefined itself as a gathering place for the entire

Golden strié walls and warmly colored textiles set a sophisticated tone in designer Nina Campbell's elegant drawing room.

family. It is decorated to be welcoming and comfortable but not, however, informal. The contemporary drawing room, like contemporary standards for polite behavior, may be a bit more relaxed than in days past, but it still retains a sense of propriety.

ARRANGING THE
FURNITURE

In terms of its organization and layout, the English drawing room bears a striking resemblance to the English garden. Both, ideally, are divided into small compartments that offer myriad opportunities for cozy conversations as well as a diversity of "vistas." In the garden, the English call these compartments "outdoor rooms" and the hedge is the principal tool for setting one space off from another. In the drawing room, a piece of furniture with strong horizontal lines, such as a sofa or a long table complemented with lamps, plants, and floral arrangements, creates the same effect.

A central conversation group generally dominates the room and typically is augmented by a number of ancillary settings, such as a tea table and chairs, or a reading chair and lamp. While this configuration is the norm in all elegant European homes, what gives it a particularly English slant is its interpretation in dwellings of more modest proportions. To the English, with their love of visually charged

Polly Devlin uses an eclectic group of comfortable armchairs to divide a large drawing room into smaller sections.

interiors, it is acceptable if not desirable to carve up even a relatively small room into nooks and crannies.

This type of furniture arrangement was not always the accepted practice. It dates back only to the 19th century, when England and other European countries finally began to release themselves from the rigid codes of social behavior that prevailed earlier. Comfort became a priority. Chairs and sofas were no longer pushed up against the walls when not in use; now they were organized in casual groupings within the room and left there, along with an assortment of small occasional tables.

To create an English feeling in your living room you must be willing to crowd a goodly number of furnishings into a relatively small space. Next, think of the possible activities in which your family and friends might engage: playing cards, enjoying tea, listening to music, and so forth. Orient your main conversation area toward a focal point, such as a fireplace or an especially attractive view. Allow the sofa to act as a "hedge," separating off a section of the room. Then position any other large pieces, such as a screen, to compartmentalize the space still further. Delineate zones for specific activities you enjoy. The objective is to create a rich "roomscape." Instead of being able to quickly absorb the layout of the room, the eye should be allowed to delight in all the intimate little vignettes that coalesce into a harmonious whole.

Just as a hedge delineates areas of a garden, designer Christophe Gollut has positioned this sofa to create zones in the drawing room.

Traditional English style is anything but sparse. Every open nook can play host to a piece of furniture. RIGHT: Designer Virginia Howard squeezes a secretaire into a small niche in her living room. BELOW AND OPPOSITE: Supplementing the main conversation areas in the center of a room should be a variety of small tables, chairs, and other objects.

One Man's Garden   Henry Mitchell

THE **WALLS**

English walls could never be characterized as shy and retiring. In the living
room, walls are every bit as rich and
vibrant as the rest of the decor. Reflecting
the English affinity for striking graphics,
walls typically achieve this effect by
employing a single brilliant color, a strong
pattern, or beautifully crafted moldings or
wooden paneling.

Regardless of how they are decorated
and adorned, walls communicate a strong
sense of structural organization. In fact,
British art historians Stephen Calloway
and Stephen Jones link the now standard
tripartite wall decoration to the revival of
classical architecture in 1613, when the
architect Inigo Jones designed the Queen's
House in Greenwich (see Resources).
The palace walls, with their dado, open
field, and cornice, related in form to the
base, shaft, and capital of the classical
columns on the building's facade. Nearly
four hundred years later, we can still
observe the same division of the wall surface in many English homes, although the
proportions have fluctuated according to
stylistic trends. Thus, the first step in re-
creating this style is to be sure your walls
at minimum are trimmed with substantial
baseboards and cornice molding. You can
evoke a specific period style, such as the

Diane Berger knows how to create an eye-
catching wall. Her hallway features a replica
of an eighteenth-century print room set against
a vibrant yellow that is characteristic of the
period. In her drawing room she has opted for
a bold, saturated red.

Proper wall trimming is important to creating a traditional English style. Substantial moldings are used in both of these rooms. Note also how additional visual interest is created by employing a brass picture rod and chains in the room at top.

Consider devoting a substantial portion of your wall space to library shelves. Books are unsurpassed in their ability to bring warmth and texture into a room.

robin's-egg blue, while the Victorians were obsessed with robust crimsons and purples. John Fowler, one of the most revered decorators of this century, introduced into the London apartment of his partner and muse, Nancy Lancaster, a sublime yellow color that epitomizes the English country look. In general, lighter colors appear in rooms intended for daytime use whereas deep, saturated jewel tones are reserved for libraries, dining rooms, and other areas where a dramatic atmosphere is desired.

For inspiration, pore over as many photographs of English interiors as you can. You may be surprised to see the frequency with which the color green appears. In countless incarnations from sea foam to olive to hunter green, the English have adored this color, perhaps because it reminds them of the sea and the garden. With regard to your own taste, take note of what colors repeatedly capture your attention and then interpret them for use in your living room.

Because of its breadth of distinctive patterns and colorways, wallpaper is an exceedingly good choice for re-creating an English atmosphere in your rooms. Floral motifs are an enduring favorite dating back many centuries to the finely detailed, hand-painted Chinese papers that were imported into England and subsequently set the gold standard for aspiring European manufacturers. (Floral motifs were prized even before wallpaper was used: in 1238, King Henry III reportedly requested that Queen Eleanor's walls be painted with flowers,

Edwardian with its deep wooden dado, by accentuating the appropriate wall detail.

If you opt for a painted finish for your walls, choose a color with verve and personality. The English have always approached color with a sense of daring. The 18th-century classicist Robert Adam often specified an exquisitely delicate

OPPOSITE, CLOCKWISE
FROM TOP LEFT:
Designer Alidad has
covered his walls with
a stunningly beautiful
hand-tooled leather.
Interior designer
Virginia Howard uphol-
stered her living room
walls with a classic
damask. Designer
George Cooper used a
combination of uphol-
stered walls and floor-
to-ceiling library
shelves in his country
home. INSET: A detail
of the upholstered
wall in Cooper's
living room.

and in 1585, Queen Elizabeth I was depicted receiving Dutch ambassadors in a room whose walls were decorated with flowers and foliage.) Today an abundant selection of floral motifs is available, ranging from the delicately beautiful patterns produced by companies such as Hamilton-Weston to the lush, artistic creations of William Morris and Liberty of London (see Resources).

If a floral motif is not to your liking, you might consider selecting a wallpaper that evokes the feeling of silk damask or one that takes its inspiration from the heraldic motifs of the 19th-century Gothic Revival style. Damask-type patterns set a marvelously sophisticated tone and impart an atmosphere of timeless elegance. Heraldic motifs hark back to the romantic images of England's ancient parish churches and medieval castles.

To maximize a wall's appearance of texture, consider upholstering it. Although perhaps a more ambitious process than wallpapering, upholstery is unmatched for the textural depth it can achieve. The walls in the drawing rooms of some of the finest homes in England have long been covered in fabric. The look recalls the leathers and tapestries that were held in high esteem during medieval and Renaissance times. In fact, tapestries were so prized that they would travel with the royal family as they moved

from castle to castle within their kingdom. Henry VIII was reported to have such a passion for collecting tapestries that he accumulated more than two thousand during his lifetime. To emulate these tapestries of old, choose a wall covering with a botanical or heraldic motif. Hand-blocked leathers (see photograph, opposite, top left) are an exceedingly expensive covering, and are usually considered only when money is no object.

Wood paneling has often played a critical role in creating splendid backdrops for the interior decor. During the Elizabethan and Jacobean periods, wall panels, usually rendered in oak, were divided into small squares. Later, in the Baroque period, paneling was more luxuriously expansive in its detailing—even though the luxury was often achieved by enhancing inexpensive wood with a faux finish such as wood graining.

During the Arts and Crafts period, walls were frequently paneled three-quarters of the way up to the ceiling, and were capped by a deep shelf or plate rack. Some Arts and Crafts designers employed the technique of dividing wall space into small squares, an echo of what had been seen in Renaissance times. In re-creating the Arts and Crafts look, feel free to paint or stain your wood. In most American homes, wood paneling is probably best reserved for a library or study.

HANGING PICTURES

No wall will ever really look English until it is liberally hung with artwork. The guideline is simple: more is more. Not only does a densely packed display of art capture the graphic look so beloved by the English, but it also offers abundant opportunities for reflecting personal taste. Lest one think that these dense arrangements are achieved pell-mell, however, it is important to note that careful planning and much pride go into the organization and hanging of works of art.

In the 18th century, when well-bred young men were sent abroad on a Grand Tour to complete their educations, they often collected works of art, especially oil paintings, from each country they visited. Back home, they typically grouped their paintings by subject, dedicating entire rooms to a single theme, such as landscapes. Hours could be spent sketching out a pleasing arrangement before the works were finally hung.

The 18th century was also a period when "print rooms" became popular. In a print room, black-and-white prints or engravings were pasted directly onto painted walls. Because arrangements of prints could be quite elaborate, noted designers such as Thomas Chippendale were often consulted for their visual expertise. The following century, the introduction of so-called dwarf bookcases allowed even more exposed wall space that could be filled with art. To add to the visual effect, pictures were suspended from gilt chains or hung against ribbons accentuated with graceful rosettes.

In your own displays, consider hanging your pictures in tiers and grouping your prints and paintings by subject. Pack them closely together and, if you desire, enhance the arrangements further with ribbons and bows or with gilt brass chains.

BELOW LEFT: Polly Devlin groups artwork featuring a variety of animal subjects in the stairwell of her country home. BELOW RIGHT: In a more formal arrangement, Ann-Louise Little has assembled black-and-white family photographs, framed them in the same style, and grouped them in a stairway. OPPOSITE: In a strikingly handsome arrangement conceived for her dining room, Diane Berger has collected a series of portraits and embellished the arrangement with sumptuous yellow ribbons.

FLOOR
COVERINGS

The English predilection for strong over-all design can clearly be seen underfoot. Distinctive carpets and rugs, in exciting patterns and colorways, are an indispensable element of the decor. In fact, long before floor carpets were in use, rich, intricate patterns were created from tile.

The most desired floor covering in English homes is now and has always been exquisitely patterned carpets from Persia and Turkey. When they were first imported to England in medieval times, Oriental carpets were hugely expensive and only the richest of the rich could afford to acquire them. Everyone else had to make do with copies. But because the British Isles have always been hospitable to sheep, wool was in ample supply. Over the centuries, English weavers produced an inspiring array of their own creations that, in varying degrees, have emulated the rich patterns of Oriental carpets.

In the 16th century, outright copies known as "English Turkey work" were attempted by hand-knotting wool on a canvas backing. In the 18th century, two large English manufactories produced hand-knotted carpets in the Turkish style as well as custom-made designs by star architects such as Robert Adam. By the 19th century, artist/craftsmen such as

Carpets from Persia and Turkey have been covering English floors since medieval times. Their highly intricate patterns suit the English penchant for visually charged interiors.

The beauty of Persian carpets and other intricately patterned hooked rugs is the way they marry with any period style. OPPOSITE: The Persian carpet enhances the opulent air that was created for this sitting room. LEFT: A well-tailored tone is anchored by this floral motif carpet.

William Morris (who had great reverence for Persian motifs) began focusing on carpet design. These days, needlepoint and hooked rugs are enjoying a revival, especially for the do-it-yourselfer.

Vying with Orientals for the title of quintessential English floor covering is sisal, or rush matting. Rushes were used as early as the Middle Ages to cover floors, both for warmth and as an ad hoc cleaning agent. Loosely strewn over the floor, they could be swept out of the house when soiled. By the time Elizabeth I ascended to the throne, people began to weave rushes into mats, which lasted longer and were easier to walk on. Since carpeting was so costly, rush mats were the only option in floor covering for many English homes. Interestingly, when carpets became more affordable, they did not always replace the rush matting, but instead were layered on top of it. This look has persisted to the present; many English lay matting on the floor and then partially cover it with one large or several small Oriental carpets.

Widespread use of carpeting became practical and affordable at the time of the Industrial Revolution, when new looms could weave wide widths (literally, "broadloom"), replacing narrow runners that had had to be sewn together to fit into a room. Predictably favoring patterns over solid colors, a sizable number of English drawing rooms sport carpets with allover designs. As in other areas of home decoration, the preferred motifs are floral, heraldic, or geometric; some feature patterns reminiscent of a garden trellis.

To create a traditional English feeling in your living room, highlight some type of pattern on the floor. Let your personal taste guide you to the particular design best suited to your home, but don't be timid! An English look is visually charged, and the floor is an important element in the ensemble.

Never hesitate to layer several carpets in a room. Often the English will layer an Oriental carpet over rush matting, but carpets themselves can also be laid one atop the other as seen here.

W I N D O W S

Surveying a range of English window treatments is a bit like gazing upon a ball-room aswirl with gorgeous ball gowns. Some might be tailored to look classically elegant while others are allowed to drift in romantic folds. Whatever the effect, all depend upon the dramatic manipulation of fabric to work their magic. To carry the fashion analogy still further, most window treatments adhere to the maxim connecting a hat and gloves to a well-dressed lady: draperies are virtually always accessorized with a pelmet and some version of the tieback.

Pelmets are a striking feature in English living rooms. They appear in myriad forms: pleated, gathered, festooned, swagged, trimmed, and adorned with serpentine tails. They can be soft and flowing or shaped by a firm pelmet board. (In the United States the word "pelmet" is generally reserved for a board that is painted or padded and both conceals the header of the draperies and crowns the window. The soft versions, created from fabric, are called "valances.") Whether soft or hard, English pelmets typically are accented by rosettes, bows, tassels, fringes, and other forms of trimming.

Almost every type of English window treatment requires a voluminous amount of fabric. Draperies should be floor length or slightly longer if you want them to

Be generous with your window treatments. In his London living room, Alidad has crowned these lush draperies with softly flowing pelmets.

ABOVE: Nina Campbell has used goblet pleats along the top of these striped drapes for a polished but not overly decorated look. RIGHT: George Cooper fashioned asymmetrical swags anchored by a choux rosette. OPPOSITE: A swag and tails should only be used on tall windows and the swag should drop approximately half of the window's height.

pool, and they should also be full. Depending upon the weight of the fabric and the treatment of the header, draperies usually require fabric that measures a minimum of two and a half to three times the width of the window. As a rule of thumb, the lighter the fabric, the more is needed to look lush and full. Draperies should be lined, and interfaced if necessary, to add body. The tone you set will depend upon the selection of the fabric: for a sophisticated urbane mood, try a silk in a solid color or a muted tone-on-tone damask. To evoke an English country

look, consider a floral chintz. And, for a tailored atmosphere, stripes are always a good choice.

The pelmet, or valance, is also critical to setting the tone. A pleated valance or swags and jabots suit a formal decorating scheme, as does a rigid pelmet that is gilded or upholstered in the same fabric as your draperies. Conversely, if you prefer a more romantic look, consider shirring the valance upon a thick pole or fashioning it with a gently scalloped silhouette. Don't indulge in frilly effects, however. While they may look very pretty in a bedroom,

Thanks to its beautiful body, ability to reflect light, and ease of sewing, chintz is prized as a fabric for window treatments. Photographer Sue Hume reflects the preference of many English in choosing a floral motif for her drawing room.

they are not appropriate for a living room.

Draperies can be an effective tool in evoking a particular era of English style. For example, the Regency period was noted for its lavish swags and elaborate "continued drapery" that connected one window to its neighbor. Serpentine jabots recall the neoclassical period, while the Victorians were enamored of fine lace curtains. If creating a period window treatment appeals to you, there are several excellent books that can provide detailed references to each period style (see Resources).

With regard to finishing touches, there are few looks more quintessentially English than the bullion fringe, seen on page 61 and throughout this chapter. Other appropriate choices would include a flat braid, cording, ruffles, and bands of fabric or ribbon such as the trim seen on the red draperies on page 62.

In English houses, draperies are often teamed with a fabric shade. In the early 19th century, when window treatments were elaborate and hardware difficult to operate, a rolling shade proved a practical solution for regulating light and furnishing privacy since curtains were simply left open day and night. The fabric shade is still popular, not only for its functional attributes but also for its contribution to the decorative scheme. The shade is often sewn up in a complementary motif or colorway, and is typically left in a semilowered position so it can be appreciated as part of the ensemble. The most popular types of shades are the standard rolling fabric shade and the pleated Roman shade; however, Austrian and balloon shades are frequently seen, as are soft shades made from sheer materials.

The English genius for embellishing their window treatments is virtually limitless. FROM TOP TO BOTTOM: Bullion fringe adorns an Austrian style blind. The beauty of green silk tails is enhanced through the use of a golden silk lining. Voluptuous choux rosettes are an excellent choice for decorating a swag type of pelmet. Coordinating fabric is fashioned into a bow to provide a finishing touch for the pelmet.

OBJECTS OF
DESIRE

The tendency to collect things is a universal human trait, one the English have raised to an art form. Houses fairly burst at the seams with all manner of things, from books to artwork to walking sticks. What sets the English apart from other cultures, however, is the extraordinary attention they lavish on small and unusual objects. Indeed the country seems collectively to be under a spell— one whose power is inversely proportional to the size and usefulness of the tiny treasures.

Tabletops, mantelpieces, plate racks, and vitrines overflow with exquisitely made little matchboxes, dinner bells, crystal inkwells, and the like. That these objects were perhaps only marginally useful in the heyday of their creation, and are certainly superfluous within the context of modern life, is beside the point. Every object is loved and displayed with great care, quite simply because it is considered beautiful, and because it connects its owner to a "golden age" when artisans were trained to impart meticulous detail to their creations. To appreciate and try your hand at this type of collecting, you must attune your eye to beauty in even its most minute incarnations. This is an endearing aspect of English culture, and one that can bring much joy to those who adopt it as their own.

Exquisite porcelain objects adorn a mantelpiece.
INSET: A rare pendulum clock.

There is only one rule to collecting objects: follow your heart. It was love at first sight for the owners of these treasures. CLOCKWISE FROM TOP LEFT: Delicate porcelain flowers crown this serving set. An elegant desktop features a mother-of-pearl letter opener, a lapis frame, and a cherished memory of a day at the Ascot. Crystal girandoles sparkle in the sunlight as winsome figures dance nearby. A sumptuously framed mirror serves as the focal point on this eclectically decorated mantel. Magnificently rendered flowers adorn a small tray. A crystal dinner bell is embellished with precious stones. A woman's cameo is inset into a box of diminutive proportions.

ART LESSON

No serious discussion of art can be undertaken in a single column of type. With this disclaimer now registered, I feel it is permissible to make the following observation: The presence of classic oil portraiture in a drawing room never fails to evoke a marvelously appealing sense of old England.

You may not be blessed with a lineage that affords you a cache of fine art documenting your bloodlines, or with an acquisition budget to rival that of the National Portrait Gallery, but that shouldn't deter you from adopting some affordable "ancestors" at auctions, flea markets, and garage sales. Have fun and dare to go large-scale. Make sure the frame is of sufficient weight to balance the portrait. And, don't take the whole process too seriously. You may bear a striking resemblance to Lady Whomever, but it will be tricky indeed staking claim to the castle in the background!

A large oil painting is the perfect embellishment above a mantel or sofa. Placed over a lowboy or console, it will pleasingly command the wall.

CLASSIC FABRICS

When the subject of English fabric is mentioned, people often reflexively think of chintz. But the pantheon of English fabrics reaches far beyond this perennial favorite. From glorious tapestries, to luxurious jacquards and velours, to lovely summer cottons and ethereal laces, England boasts a rich range of fabric styles to choose from.

The specific fabrics you select will have a dramatic impact on the atmosphere you create in your home. While there is no precise science for grouping fabrics, I have coined the following categories to give you a sense of their historical context, and of the look you can achieve by working them into your interior design scheme.

ARTS AND CRAFTS

Dramatic motifs inspired by nature's abundance and rendered in brilliantly saturated colors are the hallmark of Arts and Crafts textiles. Historically, the period also encompassed the Aesthetic style and the Art Nouveau style, and extended from about 1860 to about 1920. More than a style, Arts and Crafts was a movement. Frustrated by the declining quality of mass-produced goods, its founders and apostles, including John Ruskin and William Morris, celebrated man's creative energies, natural materials, and handmade crafts. In his textiles, Morris was renowned for his ability to combine geometric precision with naturalistic forms; flowers and leaves were designed to fit within the framework defined by devices such as trellises or scrolls. Exemplary of the Aesthetic style, London-based Liberty & Co. achieved success printing silks with motifs inspired by intricate paisley and calico designs from India. Liberty's fabrics were enthusiastically embraced by leaders of the Aesthetic movement, notably Oscar Wilde, whose notoriety proved extremely beneficial to the company.

Arts and Crafts fabrics, available in diverse weights suitable for both upholstery and draperies, adapted well to dwellings on both sides of the Atlantic. Besides Morris, other designers who worked in a similar mode were Scotland's Charles Rennie Mackintosh and American architect Frank Lloyd Wright. The interiors conceived by all were marked by the presence of hand-worked metals and woods, and by fabrics of artistic merit. Because of their sumptuous detail, Arts and Crafts fabrics are especially suited to libraries and dining rooms.

The bright and muscular designs of the Arts and Crafts period are noteworthy for their dramatic interpretations of natural forms. FROM LEFT: "Cranston," "Daffodil," and "African Marigold," all designed by William Morris and reproduced today in many different colorways by Liberty of London.

GENTLY FADED

Gently faded fabrics create a romantic and genteel mood. If you lack genuine sun-faded treasures, evoke the feeling with fabrics that arrive "gracefully aged" from the loom. FROM LEFT: A cotton sateen from the Laura Ashley Decorating Collection, "Moray" from Liberty's Stewart Collection, and "Cleaves" from Laura Ashley.

"Gently faded" is a term I use to invoke the elegant grace of an era when the civilized world made time for afternoon tea. The fabrics in this group are woven in linen or cotton and are characterized by soft color palettes and delicate floral motifs. Buttery yellow, muted rose, and palest greens and blues mingle on grounds of ivory or a sepia tone often referred to as "tea-stained." Many manufacturers are weaving these fabrics in weights suitable for upholstery and drapery.

Gently faded fabrics work best when allowed to create their own ambience. They are unabashedly romantic and don't mix easily with the strong graphics and saturated colors intrinsic to other English fabrics. It would be overbearing, for example, to place a needlepoint pillow done up in bold, bright yarns in an assertive heraldic motif atop a delicately "faded" slipcover decorated in an allover pattern of sweetly petaled cabbage roses.

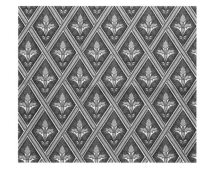

OLD ENGLAND

Old England fabrics recall the chivalry of King Arthur's Court, the splendor of the monarchy, and the authority implicit in an aristocrat's family crest. FROM LEFT: A tapestry pillow from a private collection, "Albert" from Laura Ashley, and needlework from a private collection.

Old England fabrics collectively represent the echoes of the Gothic, Elizabethan, and Jacobean periods that have been much romanticized and reprised throughout English history.

Old England motifs are hearty and robust. Often rendered in needlework, they are also eminently suited to woven textiles. Because they hark back to an epoch before artists learned the principles of perspective, most designs evoke the appearance of only two dimensions. No attempt is made to realistically render natural forms or the shadows that might be cast. Consequently, the strongest impressions made by these designs are geometric. Noteworthy among them are coats of arms, quatrefoils, and fleurs-de-lis. Colors replicate the original vegetable dyes— crimson red, indigo blue, yellow, ocher. Alternatively, they evoke strong colors that have aged, such as olive, mustard, dusty cobalt, and the like.

The breathtaking beauty and mystery of the Orient are captured in this exquisite collection from Ramm, Son & Crocker. FROM LEFT: "Charminster," "Mae East," and "Izmir." A Ramm Fabric ©.

INSPIRED BY THE ORIENT

The history of English decorative arts is inseparable from the close relationship the British Empire cultivated with the Far East. In 1601, Queen Elizabeth I granted the East India Company a charter to trade with the Orient, and since that time the British have been captivated by the exoticisms of the Far East. The country's most renowned designers, including Thomas Chippendale, even created their own "chinoiserie" lines of furnishings.

Predictably, the characters and motifs used by the Chinese and other Asian cultures had a profound influence on artisans working in the English textile trade. The silks, toiles, and chintzes that these artisans manufactured not only featured Oriental figures in their patterns, but also borrowed liberally from the Oriental interpretations of flora and fauna, especially birds.

The attention paid to bird and botanical motifs in Asian designs held such appeal for the English that some patterns continue to be produced today. Many stunning chintzes with an Oriental flair confer a sense of elegance and sophistication upon an interior, and thus work well in a formal living room.

Steer clear of traditional florals and focus on clean stripes, handsome motifs found in bespoke suits, or dark solids. FROM LEFT: "Arkwright" from Osborne & Little's Burdale Wool Collection, "Trellis," and "Cavalry Stripe," both from Laura Ashley.

SMARTLY TAILORED

There is a distinctly masculine side to English style—what one might call a Savile Row elegance interpreted for the realm of interior design. The look is, of course, brilliantly expressed in traditional British men's clubs, and was adroitly adapted to the American market by Ralph Lauren. Dark woods and worn leather upholstery are endemic to this decor, but there is also a role played by smartly tailored fabrics such as wool flannels, suede, and tightly woven linen or cotton canvas.

The focus here is on crispness; the feeling is not at all soft or romantic. Therefore, you will want to work with fabrics that emphasize clean lines. You might accomplish this by upholstering a wall in flannel, by slipcovering a couch as tautly as possible, or by selecting a handsome

Roman shade for a window treatment. Any type of accent should be equally well-tailored. A skirt on the sofa, for example, should be box-pleated; a window treatment could be capped with a solid pelmet.

Stripes, subtle jacquards, and dark solids are the motifs that best express the smartly tailored style. Colors are typically masculine; burgundy, moss, navy, and camel are just a few of your choices. The most famous tailored pattern is an English stripe called the "Regency stripe," classically rendered in maroon and cream. There is some disagreement among decorative arts scholars as to the original use of the Regency stripe—some believe it was employed principally for nonresidential use, such as in tearooms—but it adapts to all types of rooms and makes for a very smart decor.

CLASSIC CHINTZ

Chintz is a virtual icon of English style, and is loved the world over for its ability to bring the beauty of the English garden into the home, where it raises one's spirits even on the grayest of winter days. According to art historian Alan Gore, the name "chintz" comes from the Hindi term *chint*, which described a variegated-colored cloth. These painted or printed cottons—also called "calico" after the Indian city of Calicut—first came to the attention of the English when the East India Company began sailing to India to trade English wools for spices that came from the Spice Islands. The islanders protested that they were receiving little in return for their goods, so the Indians traded their own hand-blocked cotton fabrics for the spices. Although originally intended only for sale to the islanders, the cloths found their way onto English ships and became an immediate success back in England.

Today, "chintz" is a term generally reserved for glazed cottons, while "calico" usually describes unglazed cloth. Its luster and body combined with its ability to take color so well make chintz a natural choice for curtains, slipcovers, and table drapes. It is available in a wide range of motifs and colors, but florals rendered in soft hues tend to be the most widely accepted in English homes. The mood created with chintz is decidedly romantic, but never shy. Indeed, chintz has a wonderfully eye-catching personality.

Stunning detail and vibrant color make the classic floral chintz a perennial favorite of English decorators. These classic patterns are from the venerable firm of Ramm, Son & Crocker. FROM LEFT: "Iris & Geranium," "Clanfield," and "Motcombe." A Ramm Fabric ©.

IDEA NOTEBOOK

For a quintessentially traditional English look, finish upholstered furniture with **BULLION TRIM.**

Bypass the coffee table in favor of an **UPHOLSTERED BENCH** or **CHEST** (the latter offers lots of concealed storage). Pile the top high with favorite books and photo albums.

A good treatment for **LAMPSHADES** is a **SOFTLY PLEATED** fabric trimmed with fringe.

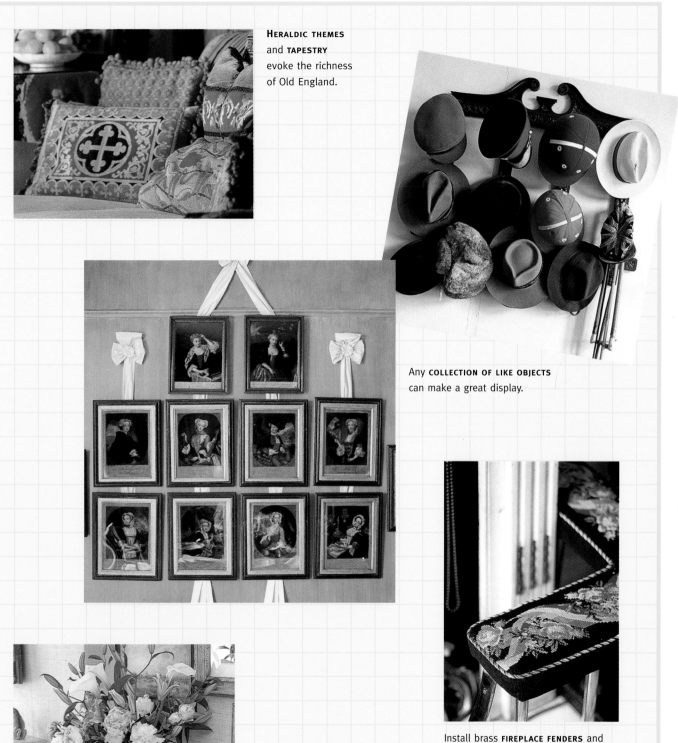

HERALDIC THEMES and **TAPESTRY** evoke the richness of Old England.

Any **COLLECTION OF LIKE OBJECTS** can make a great display.

A fresh **BOUQUET OF FLOWERS** is always a proper touch in the living room.

Install brass **FIREPLACE FENDERS** and upholster them in tapestry or leather.

LEGENDARY STYLEMAKERS

English style has been shaped over many centuries by an impressive cadre of architects and designers. Indeed, a multivolume book series would be needed to chronicle their achievements. In a quick survey, here are six of the most important, with brief sketches of their lives and work.

INIGO JONES

Inigo Jones (1573–1652) is credited with introducing the Classical Revival to England, a movement that, ironically, did not begin in earnest until a half century after his death. As a young man, Jones spent years in Italy, studying the art and architecture of Rome and the Renaissance. Leaving behind his modest roots as the son of a clothmaker, he went on to use his time in Italy as the foundation for a professional life in the rarefied environment of English court life during the reigns of Kings James I and Charles I.

At the heart of Jones's work were the classical pre-cepts embodied in the houses designed by the great 16th-century Italian architect Palladio, who in turn had studied the work of the legendary Roman architect Vitruvius. Both had published guidelines for creating structures with volumes and proportions that, they felt, were most attractive to the eye.

In 1615, Jones became the surveyor-general of the king's works and a year later began work on the Queen's House in Greenwich. This building, and other Jones designs, exemplify the Palladian theory that the only proper forms for a room are the cube, the cube and a half (e.g., 75 feet long by 50 feet wide by 50 feet high), and the double cube. Jones initiated the use of regularly spaced, narrow vertical windows evenly divided into small rectangles by slim mullions. His ceilings were coffered and sometimes featured magnificent cove moldings. His achievement was to create grandly elegant interior spaces that forever influenced English architecture.

Inigo Jones was a master of interpreting classical architecture for 17th-century England. RIGHT: A sketch for a coffered ceiling inspired by the work of the Italian architect Andrea Palladio. FAR RIGHT: The Banqueting House built between 1619 and 1622. BELOW: Wilton House was designed in collaboration with Isaac de Caux. The facade was built in 1636.

ROBERT ADAM

Scottish-born Robert Adam (1728–1792) was one of the most successful and talented decorators of the English neoclassical period. His understanding of the classical principles of design, and his ability to reinterpret them in a sublimely fresh and delicate manner, revolutionized the aesthetic preferences of the late 18th century and continued to strongly influence decoration in the centuries that followed. The eponymous Adam style, however, has come to identify an aesthetic that also embraces the influence of other luminaries of the day, such as Josiah Wedgwood and Thomas Chippendale.

Just as Adam was entering the most productive phase of his career, the ruins of Pompeii and Herculaneum were brought to light. Reports on these excavations, and a number of books depicting Etruscan and Greek antiquities, proved enormously inspirational for designers of the day. Adam borrowed and refined details from all of these sources to create a look that was as elegant as any the Western world had ever seen. Working often with his brothers James and John, Adam designed interiors in which he interpreted ancient urns, griffons, and friezes in a lighter, more delicate hand. No detail was unworthy of his attention: he specified the plans for walls, ceil-

Robert Adam left an indelible mark on architecture and the decorative arts. Much of his work was inspired by Etruscan and Greek antiquities excavated from the ruins of Pompeii. CLOCKWISE FROM TOP: Designs for a chandelier, fireplace surround, and an urn and pedestal.

ILLUSTRATIONS BY I. TERESTCHENKO

ings, carpets, furnishings, window treatments, chimney pieces, and more. He established a single aesthetic tone that carried through every room in a house, and to the exterior as well. Further, he executed these plans in lovely lucent colors such as soft sea-foam green and pale robin's-egg blue.

Both Robert and his brother James were honored with appointments to the position of architect of the king's works under King George III. The totality of Adam's vision was extraordinary, and continues to hold appeal for designers today.

Thomas Chippendale

Thomas Chippendale (1718–1779) may well be the best known and most celebrated cabinetmaker and furniture designer in history. Countless reproductions of his designs are still manufactured today. While many Americans reflexively associate Chippendale's name with the double-scroll pediment capping architect Philip Johnson's AT&T (now Sony) Building in New York City, Chippendale in fact worked in an extraordinarily wide range of styles. To suit his fancies, he borrowed liberally from classic, Chinese, and Gothic sources. For example, he did brilliant inlay work inspired by classic motifs, and introduced glazed bookcases in the Gothic mode. His Chinese-inspired creations caused a new style to be named after him, Chinese Chippendale, which featured a fretwork motif on the backs of chairs and in mirror frames.

In 1754, Chippendale published *The Gentleman and Cabinet-Maker's Director*, an illustrated treatise that was in essence a pattern book and catalog of his designs; it was the first book ever published entirely devoted to furniture design. The *Director* was a stunning success, more in fact for the influence it was to have than for the number of copies sold. Not only did the book become a bible for cabinetmakers, but it gained considerable renown abroad among luminaries such as King Louis XVI of France. In addition to offering designs for chairs, tables, bookcases, and other furniture, Chippendale ventured into some imaginative areas. For example, he demonstrated how to carve wood into pelmets that imitated the contours of heavy taffeta.

During his career, Chippendale worked in three different capacities. He designed furniture and directed a large and successful workshop with dozens of craftsmen in his employ. He served as a decorator for well-to-do English clients. And he collaborated with other decorators, such as Robert Adam, to execute furniture designs for clients. Chippendale's designs were, and remain, immensely popular in the United States.

ABOVE: Thomas Chippendale's carved window cornice was designed to crown a swag and tails. BELOW: Chippendale's ladder-back chairs were among his most produced forms. FROM LEFT TO RIGHT: The ribbon-back chair. Chippendale made many versions, often using claw and ball feet. The Chinese-back chair reflects the 18th-century appetite for objects from the Orient.

ILLUSTRATIONS BY I. TERESTCHENKO

A.W.N. Pugin's designs reflected his deep religious convictions and his belief that Gothic architecture was superior to that of the Greeks or Romans. LEFT: St. Alphonsus Church, 1844–51. ABOVE: A design for a stained glass window. BELOW: An encaustic tile design.

A.W.N. PUGIN

Augustus Welby Northmore Pugin (1812–1852) was the preeminent figure in the Gothic Revival that swept England in the 19th century. A precocious talent, Pugin was filling notebooks with studies of Gothic churches at the age of seven; at fifteen, he was invited to design Gothic furniture for the refurbishment of the state rooms at Windsor Castle.

Like many of his fellow Englishmen in the 19th century, Pugin rejected the idea of looking to classical Greece or Rome for inspiration, preferring instead to turn to his own medieval "roots." Appalled that many early attempts at reviving the Gothic style were resulting in the capricious grafting of quatrefoils or pointed arches onto structures having little connection to true Gothic architecture, Pugin decided to devote his energies to correcting such mistakes.

Pugin converted to Roman Catholicism in 1835 and became a devout practitioner of the faith. He had seen his church overshadowed by the powerful Church of England and believed that through architecture, he could restore honor and pride to England's Roman Catholics. His innate talent and his sense of purpose converged to make him the most capable practitioner of the Gothic Revival style. Where others would stop at merely copying old forms, his command of the architecture was so strong that he began to make Gothic style a vital, living option once again. His writings were regarded as textbooks of the style.

Pugin's life was as productive as it was short. Sadly, the master of Gothic architecture succumbed to a serious illness in 1852 at the age of forty.

William Morris designed this pattern, "Willow," in 1874. The fabric is still produced by Liberty & Co. Sanderson Ltd produces the wallpaper.

Morris's keen observations of thrushes in his garden gave rise to this colorful "Strawberry Thief" pattern designed in 1883.

Morris created "Poppy" in 1875. It is a good illustration of how Morris stylistically interpreted the forms of nature in two dimensions.

WILLIAM MORRIS

William Morris (1834–1896) was the 19th-century equivalent of a Renaissance man. He was a writer, painter, weaver, illustrator, typographer, philosopher, social activist, designer of furnishings and textiles, and architect. Influenced by the writings of John Ruskin, Morris was *the* great apostle of the Arts and Crafts movement in England. Believing that industrialization was contributing to a serious decline in the quality of daily life and weakening the regard for artisanship, Morris sought to revive the values that he and Ruskin believed to have been most eloquently expressed in the architecture and crafts of the Middle Ages.

Although Morris did a number of things brilliantly (for example, he was offered yet declined the position of poet laureate of England after the death of Tennyson, and he founded the enormously influential publishing venture the Kelmscott Press), he is perhaps best remembered today for his wallpaper, fabric, and carpet designs. These designs, magnificent interpretations of natural forms, were enthusiastically received and are still produced by Liberty of London and Sanderson (see Resources).

In 1861, Morris established a partnership with several fellow artists, most notably Dante Gabriel Rossetti. Most of their commissions were for works of stained glass and tile for various churches. But the partnership began to unravel several years later and finally in 1875, Morris went off on his own and founded Morris & Co. By then, his focus had turned to domestic commissions, and he entered a particularly productive period as a textile designer. The quality of work executed by his firm was exceptional, and he met with great success decorating the houses of a well-to-do and artistically astute clientele. Ironically, the "common man," whose rights Morris eloquently championed, was not able to afford his labor-intensive designs.

JOHN FOWLER

John Fowler (1906–1977) was the most influential English designer of the 20th century. In partnership with American-born Nancy Lancaster, he is credited with developing the much beloved "English country house" look. Fowler created decorative visions of a genteel and tranquil country life that were, perhaps, based more on idealized recollections and fantasies than on reality.

In 1937, Fowler became a founding partner in the decorating firm of Colefax & Fowler, which remains in existence to this day. (Nancy Lancaster bought Colefax & Fowler after World War II.) The company's hallmark style was a gracious and elegant decor that largely relied upon the effect created by sumptuous window treatments and upholstery. Copious amounts of floral chintz, a favorite fabric of Fowler's, were draped and swagged over windows, tables, and beds. The resulting atmosphere was both refined and comfortable. It was also far harder to pull off than one might imagine. Fowler's thorough understanding of English Palladianism, Regency-style window treatments, and 19th-century upholstery techniques allowed him to bring into perfect balance elements that would look hopelessly cliché or pretentious in less talented hands.

A particularly dramatic aspect of Fowler's decorating sensibility was his daring use of color. Working with Nancy Lancaster in her London home, for example, he applied a bright yellow, high-gloss paint to the walls. It was a smashing success, and is today widely emulated by decorators looking to create an English country house look. The fabrics and wallpapers developed under the Colefax & Fowler imprimatur similarly employed bold color combinations. Fowler died in 1977, but his firm continues to provide the high quality of service he mandated during his lifetime.

Collaborating with Nancy Lancaster in her London home, John Fowler created this scheme, which made extensive use of a cheerful high-gloss yellow paint. The resulting effect became a standard of the English country house look.

THE BEDROOM

Since medieval times, the English have lavished attention upon the bedroom. In the Tudor period (1509–1625), when monarchs would sometimes hold audiences in their bedrooms, magnificent four-poster beds were luxuriously draped, set on platforms, and placed in imposing rooms. The master bedroom was still accorded generous proportions in the Georgian period (1760–1830) and was located along with the key public

The bedroom is a place to be unabashedly romantic. It's the perfect setting to combine a variety of the brilliant floral chintzes for which England is renowned.

rooms on the first floor of the home. During the 19th century, the expanding middle classes reinterpreted the grandly scaled chambers of the upper classes, creating for themselves smaller but enormously inviting havens.

Today, whether in a small city apartment or a capacious country house, careful attention is still given to the decoration of the bedroom. First and foremost, it must be a peaceful and cozy sanctuary. And, in a land where the benchmarks for judging comfort are set high indeed, the bedroom is a supremely comfortable place. Appointments like chintz-covered window seats, skirted dressing tables, and pleasing collections of, say, painted tole tea caddies or botanical prints are but a few of the measures taken to ensure an inviting atmosphere.

The **BED**

Winston Churchill worked in his bed. John Lennon and Yoko Ono staged a sleep-in on theirs. Cecil Beaton spent afternoons lounging in his guest-room bed when visiting Nancy Lancaster. Suffice it to say, in England a bed is an important piece of furniture and therefore deserving of one's full attention in the matter of dressing it.

OPPOSITE: A beautiful effect is created by gathering the canopy fabric and anchoring it with a choux rosette. LEFT: Designer George Cooper has created a cozy guest room by building a rectangular frame over the head of the bed and draping it with floral chintz lined in a coordinating solid.

Four-poster canopy beds have long been cherished, and are an excellent choice for creating an English atmosphere. Back in the time of King Henry VIII, four-posters were swathed in voluminous drapes, in part to provide warmth and privacy for the sleeper and in part to conceal awkward joinery work. By Elizabethan times, however, the tools and skills of the craftsmen had evolved so dramatically that beautifully turned posts and carved testers and headboards were being created throughout the country. While stately beds for the most part continued to feature floor-length drapings at all four posts, a variation on this theme developed for other beds. Perhaps in an effort to reveal the full glory of the now beautifully turned or carved posts at the foot of the bed, floor-length drapes were gradually restricted to use only at the head. A pelmet hung from the canopy, and a "valence"—the English term for a bed skirt—completed the picture.

Before the Georgian period, walnut was used for the best beds. In the 18th century, when disease dramatically reduced the supply of this deep-hued wood, cabinetmakers turned to mahogany. A favorite treatment for these mahogany bedposts was to taper the wood as it rose toward the canopy and to decorate it with channel grooves. Today this Georgian-style mahogany four poster has achieved the status of an icon in the world of English style.

At its most romantic the four poster is dressed in floral chintz. Another pretty option is a classic toile de Jouy–type fab-

length fabric is suspended. Both offer myriad opportunities for creative self-expression. You might consider fashioning one with a straight border, a scalloped edge, undulating curves, or impressive cutwork. As with the canopy bed, the most romantic versions of the corona or half-tester are dressed in pretty floral chintzes. Trims for the draperies can range from expensive silk braid and cord to ribbons to ruffles. For a very grand effect, swags and rosettes are a magnificent alternative to a gathered fabric treatment.

A valence, or bed skirt, completes the ensemble. Even if the canopy is elaborately detailed, the bed skirt tends to be simple. The most popular version is a softly gathered skirt. However, if a tailored look is desired, a smartly finished box pleat will be used.

Certainly not every bed in England features a canopy, half-tester or corona, and bed hangings. What the bed does hope to offer the sleeper, with or without such ornament, is a feeling of sanctuary. In this regard, an often-seen feature is the upholstered headboard. Generally it is not matched by a footboard, although a bench may be placed at the foot of the bed. The upholstered headboard not only provides creature comfort but affords yet another surface that can be covered with fabric. Alternatively, a charming option for a bed head, particularly in a country setting, is to use an antique or reproduction painted headboard. These were often made from pine, then given a dark base coat and painted with sprays of delicate flowers.

LEFT: Note the decorative details of this bed. The canopy and posts feature beautiful carving. The drop of the canopy is well balanced for the proportions of the bed. The tassel trim is a good choice both for style and color. And the bedskirt is pleasantly full without being overly ruffled. ABOVE: The contours of this canopy are quite clean and tailored, but the scalloped edges and corner tassels provide just the right softening effect for the mood of the bedroom.

ric. Although these toiles are reflexively associated with France, they were in fact extremely popular in 18th-century England, and were manufactured domestically by a number of weavers. A solid fabric in a soft color may line the bed curtains at the head of the bed; the same solid fabric might also be used to create the underside of a canopy that is gathered from the four posts toward the center in a starburst effect, then trimmed with an overscaled upholstered button or rosette.

To emulate the canopy effect without bedposts, the English turn to the rectangular half-tester or to the smaller corona in a half-moon, circular, or oval shape. Both are small wooden frames affixed directly to the wall or to the ceiling over the head of the bed from which floor-

The GATHERING

Everywhere the eye roams in an English bedroom, it is met by gentle waves of fabric. All these ruffled edges and gathered drapings seem intended to recall the bounty of the English garden: the feathery ripples of a peony, the infinite scallops of the dahlia, the voluptuous, velvety folds of a rose in bloom.

There are endless opportunities for gathering fabric in a bedroom. Both bed hangings and bed skirt can be gently shirred, as can a bedspread—like the blue-and-rose-colored coverings shown here. At the window, the soft valance and the draperies can be cut rather full (perhaps two and a half times the width of the window itself) so that they fall into rich folds. Here, as on the bed, a ruffled trim may be used as an accent. Lampshades can sport a gathered flounce, as can pillow shams. Small round tables placed on either side of the bed, or a dressing table, can naturally be dressed in gathered skirts, or in plain skirts edged with a ruffle.

The more you gather and ruffle, the more feminine the bedroom will look. This, while clouds of furling fabric might be dreamy in a young girl's room, couples will need to find a tone that mutually meets their definition of a romantic bedroom.

For a cozy atmosphere, don't hesitate to incorporate gathered fabric wherever possible. THIS PAGE: Fully gathered bedskirts impart a romantic tone. OPPOSITE: A ruffled pelmet is made more romantic by its wavy contours. A throw pillow is embellished with ruffled trim.

ROOM TO **RELAX**

A charming feature of most English bedrooms is the space provided for reading, writing, or otherwise passing a bit of undisturbed leisure time. It is not unusual to find a fireplace and two sizable club chairs in the bedroom. Even where space is restricted, one might at minimum include a reading chair, a lamp, and a small table. In England, the bedroom as sanctuary is not just a romantic notion; it is considered entirely essential to a civilized existence.

While it would be ideal to have a fireplace in your bedroom plus adequate space for two overstuffed chairs, neither is indispensable to creating this atmosphere. Just be guided by the principle that if you yearn to make your bedroom a retreat, it should offer at least one option to the bed as a place to relax. Maybe you can tuck a small writing desk into a corner, or pull in a moderately sized wicker chair and ottoman. A narrow bookcase can fit almost anywhere. Alternatively, favorite books can stack on a small table or bench at the foot of the bed.

The most meaningful aspect of "a room of one's own" is the presence of materials that you enjoy in your leisure time, such as stationery, needlework, a sketch pad, and of course, books. The bedroom should reflect the fact that it is not only a place to sleep—but also a place to dream!

In her master bedroom, antique dealer Maddy Kingzett has devoted considerable space for sitting and relaxing.

A bedroom need not
be of palatial dimen-
sions to offer room for
sitting and relaxing.
Here a corner of these
moderately sized
rooms has been set
aside for a comfort-
able armchair.

ROMANTIC
WALLS AND
WINDOWS

Romantic souls rejoice! The English-style bedroom provides a haven for your spirit. Unlike the public rooms, where a measure of restraint should be exercised, the bedroom is an appropriate venue for the dreamer. Here is a land without limits, with appreciation for sprays of delicate flowers in soft hues, for shimmering chintz fashioned into furls, and for watercolor visions of the arcadian life.

For the most romantic windows, the quintessentially English fabric is a floral chintz. As a rule, draperies drop to the floor (or slightly puddle) and are usually lined with an ivory or ecru cotton sateen and interfaced to give them a pleasingly heavy hand. (Light, wispy curtains, even when fashioned from chintz, will not achieve a traditional English country look.) Each drapery panel is often trimmed along its inner and bottom hems. A classic edging is a gathered ruffle in the same or a coordinated fabric. Ribbon, tassled fringe, or bullion fringe, however, are also popular. Because bedroom draperies are usually drawn each evening, many people eschew the tieback for daytime use because it requires more fussing than modern life allows.

The great majority of English bedroom windows are dressed with a pelmet, par-

OPPOSITE: Floral curtain borders and a playful ceiling design. LEFT: For a traditional look, draperies need to be lined and interfaced.

approximately 20 to 25 percent of the curtain length. Traditional swags and jabots
will fall to about half the overall drop. The
pelmet's depth varies depending on the
fabric used, the specific treatment
employed, the height of the space, and the
atmosphere of the room. Experiment a bit
to find the look that best suits your room.

Most windows are capped by a "soft"
pelmet, or what Americans call a valance.
Rather than being upholstered to a rigid
board, the fabric is gathered, smocked or
pleated, and allowed to fall softly. The finished pelmet is typically adorned with
rosettes, bows, fringe, or another type of
trim. Books devoted to the design of pelmets and curtains are available, giving
quality information to all home decorators and providing especially useful advice
for the do-it-yourselfer (see Resources).

Like the windows, bedroom walls
assume a decidedly romantic air. This is
achieved either by the application of soft
colors—butter yellow and pale antique
rose are two pretty examples—or
through the effect created by wall coverings printed with subtle, painterly garden
motifs. In the first example, the curtains
would be made up in a printed fabric that
harmonizes with the solid wall color. In
the second example, solid-color draperies
set off a printed wall covering or, alternatively, both the draperies and the wall covering sport a motif. While the same
pattern will occasionally be used for both
draperies and wall covering, more visual
interest is generated with an interplay
between two compatible motifs.

Excessive doses of the same pattern

ticularly a pelmet cut in a lyrical serpentine form—or, for narrow windows, a single arching curve. The pelmet must be
large enough to balance the proportions
of the window and room. Nothing looks
worse than a luxuriously draped window
crowned by a skimpy pelmet. In general,
the thickest part of a curving pelmet drops
approximately a quarter to a third the
total curtain length. Straight pelmets drop

can stifle a room. When layering patterns, make sure colors are harmonious. Colors need not, however, match exactly; indeed, replication of the same hues can appear stilted and overly fussy. Instead, search for a harmony of tones and shades. For example, the draperies might be made up in a chintz featuring soft pink roses with pale green stems and leaves scattered over an ivory ground. The walls could be covered with a buttery-yellow wallpaper decorated with lacy white flowers. A rule of thumb is to feature a larger motif at the window and a smaller print on the more expansive walls. Allow the wall pattern to complement the curtain fabric rather than compete with it.

THE SPACIOUS
BATHROOM

Consistent with the English priority on comfort, bathrooms are allocated a generous portion of a home's square footage, and include furnishings beyond the functional elements of counters and cabinets. In fact, in many prewar dwellings with insufficient facilities, entire rooms were preempted and converted into bathrooms. It is not at all unusual to see a room measuring 10 by 18 feet in which an upholstered chair, a small chest, and perhaps a dressing table take gracious ease alongside the tub and vanities or sinks. The WC often occupies its own alcove or space.

The accent is on comfort in the English bathroom. Pull up an easy chair and surround yourself with your favorite art.

But it is not only the additional furnishings and space that give the English bathroom its welcoming feel; it is also the manner in which the room is decorated. Windows will often have pretty curtains made from the same types of floral chintzes that might be used in the bedroom. Quirky finds garnered from travels afar might be displayed on shelves or in curio cabinets mounted on the walls. Plants and flowers happily luxuriate in the bath's moist atmosphere. Leather wastebaskets or chests bring interesting textures into play. In short, the bathroom is considered a "living space" and its character is forged through the same types of objects and materials that might be found in any room of the house.

To create an English atmosphere in a bathroom that cannot accommodate an upholstered chair or small table, concentrate on the wall and window treatments as well as on the accessories you select. Consider painting stripes on the walls, or install a cheerful floral wall covering. Perhaps there is space to hang a small bookshelf on the wall, or a collection of straw hats. Look for unusual objects that don't require much floor space to make a statement, such as a funky antique towel stand or rack. Think of your bathroom as an intregal part of the sanctuary that the bedroom represents, and allow it to assume an equally cozy and ingratiating personality.

RIGHT: Unusual objects and artwork collected during one's travels make wonderful decorations in the bath. FAR RIGHT: Author Diane Berger placed an antique corona above her bathtub.

IDEA NOTEBOOK

To soften the mood in a bedroom, select lamp-shades that are **PLEATED** and perhaps trimmed with a **RUFFLED EDGE.**

Create a cozy bedroom nook by **LAYERING SEVERAL DIFFERENT MOTIFS** such as the variety of floral patterns and plaid seen here.

Even a small bedroom can offer a **CORNER FOR READING OR PAMPERING ONESELF.** The small-scale vanity makes this corner work.

Layer small **PERSIAN** or **KILIM** rugs **OVER RUSH MATTING** or sisal.

DISPLAY ARTWORK in dense groupings in the bath.

If you have the space, place a **COTTON-SLIPCOVERED ARMCHAIR** in the bath.

PORCELAIN PLATES make wonderful decorative touches in the bedroom or bathroom.

Don't forget to **DECORATE AT THE FLOOR LEVEL** if space permits. Porcelain pitchers, leather trunks, wicker baskets, and the like all make the bathroom more cozy.

THE NURSERY

When James M. Barrie wrote his wonderful tale about Peter Pan, he gave us much more than the character of a charming boy who refused to grow up. He also provided one of the most enchanting images of a children's nursery in literature, a magical dormitory/playroom where Wendy, Michael, and John Darling (with their beloved dog, Nana) were nourished during their formative years. Today, almost a century later, the spirit of the nursery still thrives in England.

With laudable success, the English have resisted the trend toward pushing children too quickly into adolescence. Little girls still wear smocked cotton dresses, lace-trimmed ankle socks, and Mary Jane shoes. Little boys wear crisp white shirts (with Peter Pan collars), navy blue or gray flannel shorts, and T-strap leather shoes. Children are encouraged to engage in games of make believe. "Tea" is served in miniature cups to guests who—or which!—often are invisible to adult eyes. Diminutive playhouses, called "Wendy houses" after Peter Pan's playmate, grace the back gardens of many English homes. Old trunks filled with dress-up clothes await the powerful imaginations of pirates and princesses in bedrooms and playrooms in every corner of Great Britain.

The value placed on childhood is reflected in the toys one finds in many English homes. The majority of playthings are built to last: trains made of wood, push toys made with sturdy metal frames and wheels, and doll clothes knit from good woolen yarn. In fact, it is quite normal to see children playing with the toys that once belonged to their parents—and their parents before them. Renowned author Evelyn Waugh used the longevity of beloved childhood possessions to great emotional effect in his novel *Brideshead Revisited* when he created the character of Lord Sebastian Flyte, who rarely parted company with his very special teddy bear, Aloyisius.

While toy trains, children's teas, and Wendy houses rank quite high on the list of favorite toys and activities, more rambunctious pursuits, especially for boys, are certainly not forsaken. A cricket bat, rugby ball, and a football (or soccer ball, in the United States) are indispensable elements in a child's collection. Fertile imaginations are by no means mutually incompatible with budding athleticism!

Whether sprinting between wickets or cozying up with a copy of *Winnie-the-Pooh* or *Peter Rabbit*, being a child is an important role in English family life. Great care is taken by parents to make sure that a special space is set aside, be it an entire room or just a quiet corner, where a child can indulge in imaginative pursuits with an unbridled sense of wonder.

Lilly Barton is an exceptionally discerning hostess. Her bunnies and bears are served only the finest imaginary teas and biscuits. INSET: Some cups are too heavy for small bears and a hostess is called upon to lend a helping hand.

English children like
Harry Elliott and Ned
Barton start early on
mastering the coun-
try's favorite sports:
cricket and rugby.

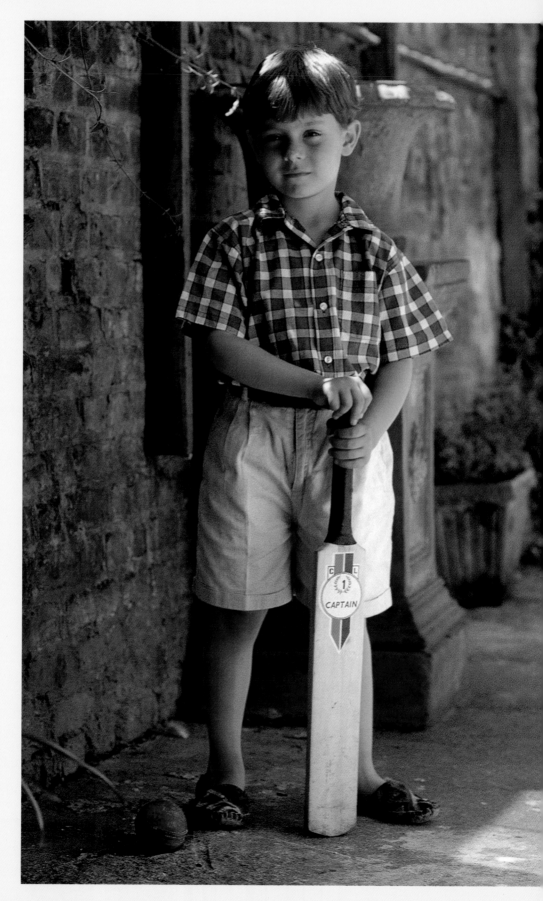

ABOVE: Emily and Katie Kingzett are joined by neighbor Victoria Goodhew for a children's tea. In England where the tradition of afternoon tea is revered, children are treated to their own special version, offering many of the same sandwiches and sweets, but served in a setting scaled down to their size. In the background is the girls' "Wendy house," the preferred term for a small playhouse. LEFT: From dollhouses to stuffed animals to countless books, there is a conspicuous lack of battery-powered objects in the nursery. The goal is to actively engage a child's imagination. RIGHT: Lacking space in the garden for an outdoor playhouse, Ann Goodhew designed her own indoor version of a Wendy house in the children's nursery. A facade was constructed to conform to the dimensions of the dormer room, complete with its own working front door.

One of the most striking elements of the English nursery is the enduring quality of the toys and books that are enjoyed by the children. It is common to see stuffed animals that belonged to parents and even grandparents. Wagons and trains are well crafted and made from wood. Beloved classics like Beatrix Potter's Peter Rabbit find their way into every generation's heart. Even the clothing worn by the children has changed little in style and is made well enough to be enjoyed by younger brothers and sisters. (See Resources.)

THE DINING ROOM

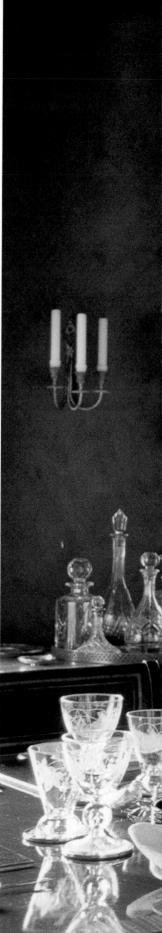

In the 1994 film adaptation of Kazuo Ishiguro's novel *Remains of the Day*, the acclaimed British actor Sir Anthony Hopkins portrays an English butler. In one scene, set in a sumptuous dining room, Hopkins meticulously measures the position of each piece of flatware, conferring an impeccably tailored air to the room.

The quintessential English dining room does, in fact, have a carefully constructed and handsomely formal

In Andrew and Helen Kilpatrick's dining room, dark, rich colors, elegant fabrics, and a splendid table setting coalesce into a very polished atmosphere.

atmosphere. It is the most masculine of all the public rooms—with the possible exception of the library—and still resonates with echoes of times in which gentlemen lingered around the table after the ladies had retired to the drawing room.

CREATING ATMOSPHERE

The smartly tailored look of a traditional English dining room is created first and foremost with bold, daring color. In the 18th century, for example, scarlet and crimson were considered very posh colors for this room. This sentiment persisted into the 19th century when, according to historians Alan and Ann Gore, "red in all tones was the colour in general use for dining rooms and libraries." Even today, intense hues of red are embraced with enthusiasm. Consider painting your walls in a strong color you particularly like; if you enjoy an extra shimmer at evening dinner parties, choose a paint in a high-gloss finish or wax and buff the walls after painting them. Alternatively, install a damask fabric or a wall covering embossed or printed with a damask motif; when rendered in a dramatic hue, either one will create a stunning effect.

Beyond dramatic wall colors, strong architectural details like crown molding and paneled wainscoting impart a crisp, masculine feeling to the dining room.

Stylist Christine Knox has adroitly paired the visual texture of floor-to-ceiling library shelves with the warmth of a deep red wall color.

These are elements that can easily be added to even the most banal of spaces. Ideally, an English-style dining room features a pleasing fireplace, but this element admittedly is not as easy to retrofit as are moldings and trim. If you are ambitious and have the space, you can build out a wall a bit to simulate a chimneypiece, affix a mantel to it, and construct a "firebox" within the cavity. Another possible remedy for rooms lacking architectural interest is to construct a floor-to-ceiling bookcase along an interior wall. As seen in the photo on page 116, the profile of the wood and the presence of so many books create a strong and very agreeable atmosphere.

A third element in creating the right mood is the selection of furnishings. As we have seen, the English aesthetic favors dark woods; thus it is quite understandable that many British consider the *non plus ultra* of a fine dining room to be a Georgian-style mahogany table, with its slim profile, apronless top poised on a double-pedestal base and polished to a

Strong decorative statements work well in traditional English dining rooms. TOP: These window treatments and the room's color palette are both pleasingly assertive. RIGHT: The daring use of color and large-scale art give this dining room a wonderful character.

In part, the masculine air in the English dining room comes from the rich presence of wood, marble, and other deep tones. Each of these three rooms are made more dramatic by the juxtaposition of fine crystal and silver against the polished surface of the tables.

dazzling shine. Mahogany or other dark wood chairs boasting some type of pierced splat, shield, or Regency-style back design encircle the table. Lastly, the room would include a handsome breakfront or sideboard, similarly waxed and buffed. Certainly, styles other than Georgian are admired and acquired, but all rely on the abundant presence of deep-hued woods to establish the atmosphere of the room.

Other appointments in the room, like the rug and the lighting, should follow the tone established by the major furnishings. Fussy or overly feminine details such as a ruffled pelmet or a lampshade with frilly trim will look out of place.

Silver Jubilee

Sterling silver has long been considered the most prestigious of table decorations. Until the 18th century, sterling was inextricably linked to two status-conferring luxuries: tea caddies and candlesticks. Tea was such an expensive commodity in 17th-century England that the mistress of the house would not allow her servants to prepare this special brew, preferring instead to attend to it herself. The rare beverage was served in a silver teapot and often stored in a silver tea caddy that remained under lock and key (the mistress of the house kept the key on her person) when not in use. At that time, beeswax candles were also prohibitively costly, and would remain so throughout the 18th century. Most families made do with straws of dried rush dipped in animal fat, or tallow candles made from rendered animal fat. Those who could afford the pricey version of this light source also possessed an appropriately luxurious holder—a silver candlestick.

Although out of reach to all but the elite, the crowning glory of a superbly decorated dining room—and an important part of any great inheritance—was a substantial collection of silverware. The aristocratic dining room was lavished with many spectacular creations in silver, most of them engraved with the monograms or coats of arms of the family. But in the

Whether family heirlooms or flea market finds, silver objects are the center of attraction on the English dining table.

1770s, silversmiths in Sheffield created "Sheffield plate," a process by which a veneer of silver could be fused to copper. Plating required only a fraction of the silver found in traditionally crafted pieces, and thus allowed middle-class families to emulate the wealthy in their decor.

The aesthetic appeal of silver in the English dining room has never waned. While the quality and purity of a collection varies according to the means of the owner, silver is still integral to the decoration of the dining room. While entertaining guests, silver wares are brought out in force, including not only flatware, candlesticks, and serving dishes but also myriad accent pieces such as salt cellars and pepper shakers, bud vases and butter dishes. At other times, a beautiful collection of silver—such as a tea service—can be kept out on the sideboard. To enhance this English effect in your own home, consider displaying silver-framed photographs and other purely decorative silver objects in addition to service items such as bowls or trays.

Silver objects are worth the upkeep they will need. They will of course tarnish when exposed to the air. It is best to wear plastic or cotton gloves when polishing, since contact with rubber gloves can promote tarnishing.

How to Set
The Table

In the lexicon of fine quality tablewares, England claims some of Europe's oldest and most distinguished entries: Wedgwood, Royal Worcester/Spode, Minton, and Royal Doulton, to name just a few. Great pride has always been taken in "laying a proper table" (in England one *lays*, not *sets*, a table), and that practice continues today. Not surprisingly, given the appealingly formal tone of the traditional dining room, English tables maintain a classical sense of order in their decoration.

TABLE DRESSING

With all the attention given to a collection of silver, it is only natural that the English hostess would want to put it in the best light. Since gleaming silver shows beautifully against dark wood, a table is often not covered by a tablecloth. It is perfectly proper to set the dinner plate or charger directly upon the table. If a hostess wishes to protect the finish on the tabletop from heat, moisture, or potential scratches, a rigid *table mat* is inserted under the dinner plate or charger. Table

OPPOSITE: London designer Alidad prefers an elegantly tailored setting. Small mats under the dinnerware protect, yet don't obscure, the beautiful wood. The traditional porcelain pattern features just a small medallion, reflecting the purist's view that food should be presented on a white surface. Napkins are folded into clean rectangles. LEFT: Diane Berger opts for a slightly less formal tone with her classic Blue Willow china and cobalt glasses.

RIGHT: As an alternative to table mats, the English frequently choose white linen placemats for their tables. Napkins are generally handled in a no-fuss manner; they are folded neatly and placed on the bread plate, or to the side of the dinner plate if no bread plate is used. BELOW: This table follows strict English tradition; that is, the dessert fork and spoon are not placed above the plate.

mats are usually made from wood decorated with scenic or botanical prints and then lacquered; their undersides are cushioned with felt so they cannot damage the table. (Note the dark green table mat on page 115.) Alternatively, a white linen place mat may be used in place of the rigid table mat.

For those whose table, in the words of *Debrett's New Guide to Etiquette and Modern Manners*, "boasts a less-than-perfect surface," a tablecloth makes excellent sense. White linen damask is considered a classic, though by no means mandatory, choice. (So as not to suggest that every tablecloth is camouflaging a flawed table, it must be mentioned that some people prefer white linen formality regardless of the table's condition.) For dining in a conservatory or out in the garden, nothing could be more perfectly suited to the occasion than a cotton chintz in a floral motif.

Table napkins can either be laid directly upon the table mat (if the dinner plate has not been set out ahead of time) or on the bread plate as seen in the photo at left. If a bread plate is not used, the napkin may be placed just to the left of the dinner plate. Generally, the English prefer just a simple fold for the dinner napkin; overly intricate or eye-catching measures are frowned upon.

PLACE SETTINGS
The number of implements to be placed at each setting will depend on the number of courses and the food to be served. Forks are placed to the left of the dinner plate, tines facing up, in the order in which they

will be used. Knives (blades facing inward) and spoons (bowls facing up) are placed to the right, also in order of use. The arrangement should look balanced and evenly spaced.

If they are following strict tradition, the English do not place the dessert fork and spoon above the dinner plate. All of the implements are laid to the proper side of the dinner plate. However, after so many centuries of contact with their neighbors across the Channel, many elegant dinner tables are in fact set with the "pudding" fork and spoon placed *à la française*, or above the plate.

Although the beauty of the dark wood table is highly appreciated, for some occasions an English hostess will prefer a classic white tablecloth. Above: Using her own "Mayfair" china design, Nina Campbell creates a lively, almost playful tone. Frolicsome rabbit-shaped salts and peppers and delightful decorative glass spheres enhance the mood.

TABLEWARE

England manufactures exquisitely beautiful porcelains and pottery. To understand the various terms used, such as "ironstone" or "bone china," one must first understand the essential differences between porcelain and pottery. While both are made from clay, porcelain—also known as china—is made from white clay only. It is fired at extremely high temperatures, rendering it flawlessly smooth and translucent at its delicate edges. Pottery—often called earthenware—is made from red clay, and can be fired at lower temperatures. When earthenware is fired at temperatures high enough to fuse the clay into an impervious, vitrified mass, it becomes stoneware. Ironstone was a trade name patented in 1813 by C. J. and G. Miles Mason for their version of stoneware that purportedly included ironstone slag, among other mineral additives. While not technically true porcelains, the Masons' Ironstone, and the stonewares of distinguished factories such as Spode and Royal Doulton, closely approximated the qualities of true china.

In the second half of the 18th century, English chinaware factories began experimenting with a new type of porcelain called "bone china." Bone ash, or calcium phosphate, was incorporated into the recipe for porcelain developed in ancient China. The result was a hybrid product that approximated the appealing pure white body of the Chinese porcelains (known as "hard-paste" porcelain) yet offered a luminous quality close to the superior translucence of "soft-paste" porcelains developed in Europe, the most famous of which was made in Sèvres, France.

The vast majority of English dinner services feature either delicate fruit, floral, or bird motifs, "stately" patterns such as a crown encircled by decorative scrolls, or transfer-printed pictorial motifs such as the Blue Willow pattern adapted by Thomas Minton from a Chinese landscape. White is by far the preferred ground color for a design, conferring a clean and classical air to the table.

It is by no means necessary or preferable to use the same dinner service throughout the meal. Many hostesses enjoy choreographing a number of different china patterns throughout the evening. In some homes, a single service may be used up through the main course, with the cheese and dessert courses presented on special plates.

Fine bone dinnerware is revered for the purity of its white ground color and its luminosity. This elegant pattern, manufactured by Spode, is known as "Lancaster" and was first recorded in 1897.

It is perfectly acceptable to use a mixture of colored, cut, and clear crystal at the same setting.

CRYSTAL

A stroll through the crystal department of Harrod's, London's most famous department store, reveals an awe-inspiring selection of glassware. Quite strikingly, a number of models feature stems in which a single or double spiral of air is encapsulated. According to art historian Steven Parissien, these "air twists" date back to the mid-1700s when glass was taxed by weight. Thus, not only were drinking glasses designed to be lighter to reduce the tax, but as the air twists were perfected, the designs also became more elegant and refined.

The English table continues to feature elegant, often engraved, stemware. The position of the glasses follows that of European and American settings: they are placed in order of use above the right-hand side of the place setting, with the water goblet placed to the left of the wineglasses and over the center of the dinner plate. Most settings include a glass for white wine, a glass for red wine, and the water goblet.

For formal occasions a champagne flute will be placed just to the right of the white wineglass. (*Debrett's* judges champagne coupes rather harshly: "Champagne is served in fluted glasses and not in 'boats,' which are downmarket, impractical and associated with elderly starlets.")

FLOWERS

Rare indeed is the English table that does not feature a floral centerpiece. It is the perfect occasion to display the gardener's prowess, or in winter, when the florist is the principle resource, to provide an emotional lift until spring comes round again. As is true anywhere, the centerpiece should be low enough for diners to easily converse across the table, and should not be so fragrant as to interfere with the enjoyment of the food.

The tone of the centerpiece varies with the occasion. All English bouquets, from a handful of assorted blossoms arranged in a simple creamware bowl to an artful array of summer roses collected in a silver vase, display a sense of freshness and spontaneity.

Flowers are most often mixed, with small selections of different types. Slender sprays and bits of greenery poke their way up through rounder, plumper blossoms. Great care is taken not to force an arrangement into an unnaturally contrived form but rather to emulate the casual, tumbled look of the garden.

The mood of the bouquet should match the mood of the meal. If you are creating a centerpiece for a luncheon, a playful group of flowers such as poppies, violets, or even daisies might be used. If you are planning an elegant dinner, a more appropriate bouquet will include such botanical "stars" as roses, snapdragons, or lilies.

A WORD ABOUT **TABLES** AND **CHAIRS**

In selecting tables and chairs for your dining room, it is helpful to understand what attributes give a piece its "English feel." On this page are the profiles of several models that have achieved iconic status in the traditional English dining room. While authentic examples of these pieces still exist, many good-quality reproductions are available at prices affordable to the Anglophile on a less than royal budget.

Regency chairs are distinctive for their sabre legs and scrolled arms. Their sophisticated and graceful designs were all the rage in the early part of the nineteenth century. Many variations exist on the Regency chair: the scrolled arm can curl toward the back or front. The back may feature two horizontal pieces, as in this sketch, a top rail paired with a gently curving and horizontally positioned "X" shaped back, or even a padded horizontal back splat.

Thomas Chippendale, regarded by many as the Shakespeare of English furniture-makers, designed endless variations on his splat-back chair. Many of his models, like this one, featured sinuous forms. Typical leg shapes for chairs at the mid-point of the eighteenth century looked like this one: gently curving legs, often embellished with carvings, taper gradually down to the foot. These chairs have sturdy, broad seats and will comfortably accommodate their occupants.

George Hepplewhite was part of the Golden Era of furniture design in 18th-century England. He is most closely associated with the shield-back chair. This particular design is known as a Prince of Wales' feather motif. The legs are generally straight and are particularly appropriate if you favor the Neoclassical style. Since its creation, the shield-back chair has been extensively reproduced.

Thomas Sheraton was an important contributor to the Adam style, although sadly he was not to achieve fortune through his work, and in fact died in poverty. His preference in chair design was for square backs and upright splats as shown in this sketch. The legs are generally straight and, in the back, curve away from the chair. The clean, strong lines of his designs make them very appropriate for a dining room with a masculine tone.

A George III pedestal table rendered in rich mahogany is considered by many to be the Rolls Royce of English tables. Variously described as Late-Georgian or Regency, its distinctive features are an apronless (or shallow-aproned) top and the gracefully curving legs of its pedestals. It is an elegant and masculine design in addition to being quite comfortable. The absence of an apron makes it easy to use different types of chairs, such as the Queen Anne style shown here, whose seat heights might vary. The diner can cross his legs or move about without fear of striking the table.

IDEA NOTEBOOK

Instead of a tablecloth or traditional linen place mats, consider **WOVEN TABLE MATS** or **CHARGERS** set directly on the table.

Group and display **FINE CRYSTAL DECANTERS** in the dining room.

MAHOGANY IS THE QUINTESSENTIAL WOOD for traditional English dining tables and chairs. Note the **OPEN** design of the **CHAIR BACKS.**

When following traditional English protocol, silverware is **PLACED TO THE SIDES OF THE PLATE ONLY,** never above.

When arranging flowers for the table, **KEEP THE MOOD SOFT AND NATURAL.**

As you extend your collection of silver beyond place settings and candlesticks, look for small objects like **SALT CELLARS, PLACE CARD HOLDERS, AND ORNAMENTAL OBJECTS.**

A Time Line of English Style

Understanding what is meant by terms like "Jacobean style," "Georgian style," or "Arts and Crafts style" can be tricky. The human spirit, the source of all decorative innovations, is far too capricious to travel along well-defined tracks or obey distinct lines of demarcation when making transitions from one period to the next. Practical barriers are also unavoidable; one doesn't simply sweep the house clean of all furnishings each time a new monarch ascends to the throne. Old pieces remain, new pieces are added, and only over time do the dominant characteristics of a period style come into focus.

A comprehensive study of English period styles would fill several volumes, so I have taken the liberty of devising a thumbnail sketch of sorts to illuminate their salient points. In the interest of providing as concise a guide as possible, I have compressed several discrete periods into larger, longer eras.

ILLUSTRATIONS BY I. TERESTCHENKO

GOTHIC

Time line:
Late 12th century to beginning of 16th century

Other style names used during epoch:
Early English, Decorated, Court Style, Perpendicular

Monarchs:
Richard I, John, Henry III, Edward I, II, III, Richard II, Henry IV, V, VI, Edward IV, V, Richard III, Henry VII

Mileposts:
The Magna Carta is signed in 1215. Parliament is formed and begins meeting regularly in late 1200s. Bubonic plague (the Black Death) strikes in 1348. War of the Roses ends in 1485, bringing relative peace and stability under Henry VII.

Architectural characteristics:
Pointed arch, rib vault, flying buttress

Decorative devices:
Ogee, trefoil, quatrefoil, carved foliage and rosettes, fleur-de-lis and heraldic motifs

Interior details:
Tapestries and wainscoting used for decoration and insulation. Large windows delineated by tracery; elaborate decorative stone or wood work separating panes of glass. Furniture is relatively sparse. Open-shelved cup-

boards placed in the hallway to display a family's few dinnerwares. Only the rich own beds. Most seating consists of benches; tables are simply planks on trestles.

TUDOR/ELIZABETHAN/JACOBEAN

Time line:
1509–1625

Other style names used during epoch:
Renaissance

Monarchs:
Henry VIII, Edward VI, Mary I, Elizabeth I, James I. (Followers of James I were called "Jacobites," hence Jacobean style)

Mileposts:
Henry VIII ascends throne in 1509, breaks with Roman Catholic Church in 1534. Shakespeare is born in 1564. London Stock Exchange founded 1571.

Architectural characteristics:
Italian Renaissance influences such as classically inspired friezes. Facades are very geometric and linear. Tall rectangular windows are divided

into many small squares. Buildings are striking for the impression they give of compact horizontality.

Decorative devices:
Many Gothic forms such as carved foliage and tracery persist. Strapwork—carved ornamental patterns of inter-

lacing bands resembling leather straps—becomes popular. Grids formed by mullions and transoms are used for paneling as well as windows.

Interior details:
Furnishings, quite heavy, are generally rendered in walnut, feature elaborate carving and turning.

CLASSICAL/PALLADIAN/EARLY GEORGIAN

Time line:

1625–1760

Other style names used during epoch:

Inigo Jones style (see page 78), Baroque, Chinoiserie, Restoration, Queen Anne

Monarchs:

Charles I, II, James II, William III, Mary II, Anne, George I, II

Mileposts:

English Civil War breaks out in 1642. In 1649, led by Oliver Cromwell, England becomes a republic for eleven years. Isaac Newton defines law of gravitation in 1684. Jonathan Swift writes *Gulliver's Travels* in 1726.

Architectural characteristics:

Inigo Jones builds the Queen's House in Greenwich, bringing classical disciplines of order and proportion to England. Facades are more elegant with regularly spaced, vertical windows.

Decorative devices:

After his exile on the Continent, Charles II imports a taste for Baroque decoration. Interiors of classic buildings are splendidly embellished with sinewy details such as scrolls, crowns, shells, and dolphins.

Interior details:

Interiors become lighter and more elegant in feeling. Trade with China introduces Oriental motifs. Cabinetmakers' skills reach a new high. Many consider this the golden age of the English interior.

GEORGIAN/ADAM/REGENCY

Time line:

1760–1830

Other style names used during epoch:

Neoclassical, Mid-Georgian, Rococo, Late Georgian. (See Robert Adam, page 79; Thomas Chippendale, page 80.)

Monarchs:

George III, IV

Mileposts:

James Hargreaves invents the spinning jenny in 1764. James Watt patents the steam engine in 1769. American colonies break away in 1776. George III declared insane in 1810.

Architectural characteristics:

Classical influences prevail, and Robert Adam takes them to a new level of lightness and delicacy. Use of windowed domes to bring in more light expands under Sir John Soane. Great crescents, or semicircular assemblages of town houses, such as Oxford Circus in London and the Royal and Camden crescents in Bath, are erected.

Decorative devices:

Classical motifs such as garlands, scrolls, and urns remain popular, but Etruscan motifs inspired by the excavation of Pompeii become all the rage.

Interior details:

Robert Adam brings a sumptuous new color palette of rich, deep colors as well as pale pastels to the English house. Cabinetmakers Thomas Chippendale, George Hepplewhite, and Thomas Sheraton usher in a golden age of furniture, especially for chairs such as the saber-legged Regency model and the lyre-back and medallion-back models. (See page 133.)

VICTORIAN

Time line:
1830–1860

Other style names used during epoch:
Norman Revival, Tudor Revival, Gothic Revival (see A.W.N. Pugin, page 81), Italianate, Early Victorian, High Victorian

Monarchs:
William IV, Victoria

Mileposts:
Manchester-Liverpool railroad opens in 1830. Victoria ascends to the throne in 1837. In 1847, Charlotte Brontë publishes *Jane Eyre* and her sister Emily publishes *Wuthering Heights*. Charles Darwin publishes *On the Origin of Species by Means of Natural Selection* in 1859.

Architectural characteristics and decorative devices:
The Industrial Revolution and unprecedented prosperity result in an architectural free-for-all. Every style imaginable is reprised. The only common thread is enormous amounts of exterior and interior decoration, made possible by new tools such as the steam-

powered jigsaw used to cut "gingerbread" decoration. Cast-iron facades for buildings are introduced.

Interior details:
Densely and ecclectically furnished rooms. Penchant for tufted upholstery. Rich layering of patterns. Much furniture is highly decorated, with many pieces featuring mother-of-pearl inlays. Window treatments are dramatic, with arched lambrequins trimmed with heavy fringe. Mass-production techniques tend to result in a drop in quality.

ARTS AND CRAFTS/AESTHETIC

Time line:
1860–1920

Other style names used during epoch:
Queen Anne, Art Nouveau, Adam Revival, Georgian Revival, Edwardian, Art Deco (see William Morris, Liberty of London, page 82)

Monarchs:
Victoria, Edward VII, George V

Mileposts:
Prince Albert, Victoria's consort, dies in 1861. Oscar Wilde publishes *The Picture of Dorian Gray* in 1891. Queen Victoria dies in 1901. World War I breaks out in 1914.

Architectural characteristics:
Inspiration comes from the past, particularly the Gothic era, or from the vernacular styles of rustic country cottages. Asymmetry reigns; half-timbers widely used on facades. Roofs tend to display high front or side gables.

Decorative devices:
Ornament becomes an integral part of structure: ceramic tiles form a design on a building's facade; strapwork-inspired hinges installed on doors; stained glass used for windows. Many motifs take the form of stylized plants, flowers. Japanese prints are a major design inspiration for Aesthetic interiors.

Interior details:
Philosopher writers such as John Ruskin and William Morris urge people to put artisanship and quality ahead of pure consumerism. An emphasis is put on natural materials and craftsmanship. Use of wood, especially oak, is emphasized. Great attention is paid to joinery; many built-ins are used to keep the living area open and spacious in feeling.

THE GARDEN

"It is our art form," says Andy Garnet, as he sits in the garden of his Somerset home and reflects on this quintessential feature of the English landscape. "The Italians have their opera and the French their cuisine, but for the English, it will always be the garden."

The English have always groomed their land. When Roman emperor Claudius invaded Britain in A.D. 43, he found a landscape already ordered by tidy hedgerows. In the

The garden at Long Barn, a residence formerly owned by Vita Sackville-West, who went on to create the renowned garden at Sissinghurst. INSET: Maxime Magan.

ensuing centuries, the reputation of the British as avid and accomplished gardeners grew to majestic proportions, fueled by the work of such renowned garden architects as Lancelot "Capability" Brown, Russell Page, and Gertrude Jekyll, and the practiced amateur Vita Sackville-West, whose white garden at Sissinghurst is a must-see on any garden tour.

Gardening is a lifelong passion for the English. After spending more than forty years artfully sculpting a magnificent yew hedge on her Kent estate, eighty-year-old Maxime Magan decided to start a new hedge on a different section of her property. "My husband told me I was crazy starting a new hedge at this phase of life," she said, "but I told him I had no choice—this is the only phase of life I have."

Magan, like most English gardeners, believes that the beauty of gardening is to be found in the process, not simply in its outcome. A gardener is a temporary custodian of his or her little plot of land. Planting and tending a garden is an investment for future generations, not a project to "finish" before the end of the season. This is not to diminish the temporal pleasure of savoring fragrant roses on a warm June evening, but rather to keep the relationship between man and nature in proper perspective.

Establishing contours is an essential requirement of the English garden, and the hedge is the principle tool for achieving this. But the tone set by the hedge can vary widely. These are the gardens of, CLOCKWISE FROM TOP LEFT, Long Barn, Maxime Magan, Alison Gibbs, Long Barn.

OF STRUCTURE AND SELF-EXPRESSION

English gardens share a great deal in common with English dinner parties. Established rules of order are cheerfully observed, but never so rigidly as to preclude the opportunity for self-expression. The dinner guest maintains a quiet, dignified tone, all the while telling a wickedly mischievous story. The gardener designs and constructs a proper garden framework, all the while indulging her or his every botanical fantasy.

The basic requirement of the English garden is to establish boundaries and contours; this is achieved with a system of hedges and fencing. In the most elaborate and mature examples, thick, impeccably manicured yew hedges will hem in the garden while topiary "newel posts" define important junctures and corners. Younger gardens will by necessity rely on fencing until trees, shrubs, and hedges have a chance to grow. Ideally, hedges, gates, and mature trees converge to frame a key view. This defining structure can be very formal and geometric in appearance, echoing the straight lines and perfect circles found in Renaissance Italy, or they may be somewhat softer and more informal, featuring undulating curves. As English gardening expert Penelope Hobhouse says, "Sometimes the greatest artistry lies in creating a structure so subtle that visitors notice its power only when you decide to show your hand."

Hedges and fences create a backdrop for paths and borders encircling modest expanses of lawn. A century ago, the Edwardian paradigm called for long stretches of perfectly trimmed lawn, sweeping toward bucolic points of focus, such as a graceful old oak, a bridge, or even a garden "folly," and surrounded by beautiful herbaceous borders. Of course this type of garden demands an enormous staff and an inexhaustible maintenance budget—both rare in modern life. In the 20th century, gardens were scaled down to human dimensions; most English gardeners assume complete care for their gardens. (It is interesting to note that in England the "lawn" is part of the garden, while in the United States, the word "garden" often describes the portion of the property, other than the lawn, that is under specific cultivation.)

Within each bed, an owner expresses his or her personal vision of beauty. Some gardeners like to create small islands of a single color, and will plant masses of lavender and rosemary, for example, for the similar purple hue of their blossoms. Or they are excited by the possibilities of growing plants with particularly striking foliage, like the artichoke. Others attempt challenges like nurturing a knot garden with its interlocking chain of shrubs. Whatever their particular passion, gardeners agree on three priorities in shaping the gardenscape: a pleasing sense of texture, harmonious groupings of color, and planting beds with attention to the proper proportions, especially of height and depth.

To create an English style garden, one must take the long-term view. It has taken Maxime Magan forty years to nurture and sculpt the hedges seen above. Now with her grandchildren in mind, Magan has just planted a new hedgerow.

BEDS AND BORDERS

Herbaceous borders and flower beds are central to the individuality and character of every English garden. Aesthetically, a border should appear soft and billowy, with mounds of leafy and flowering plants that increase in height as they progress from front to back in the border.

Paradoxically, this soft and billowy look is achieved by dense, aggressive planting. In addition, planting is done to cycle the peak weeks of flowering specimens, so that borders remain vibrant all season. Colors and textures are repeated throughout the border to unify it visually from one end to the other.

Borders tend to be generous in depth, in the belief that—just as overscaled furniture can make a room appear more welcoming—ample borders are visually pleasing. Paths between borders are kept quite tidy. They tend toward classically straight lines, and are most often composed of evenly laid fieldstone, fine gravel, or closely cropped grass.

CLOCKWISE FROM TOP LEFT: An interesting contrast of a tightly trimmed yew border and a softer border. A brick wall has been used as the defining border. A classic arrangement of a tidy grass path bisecting two borders. Note the gradually increasing height of the plants as they move toward the hedge. Good border design incorporates soft, billowy forms. Beautifully proportioned borders.

FRAMING THE VIEW

A well-framed vista is the mark of good garden composition. A vista, however, is not limited to gardens with sweeping views of arcadian splendor. Even the most modest of gardens can include a nicely framed niche or a quiet corner.

The framing of a view is based on the axial planning system put forward by the ancient Romans. The eye, they felt, should be led down an orderly path with some type of visual reward at the end—a small statue, perhaps, or a bench. The visual corridor that serves to usher the eye may comprise many things: a parallel row of hedges, a path between two borders, a circular cutaway in a gate, or a pair of stone columns, for example.

While a sweeping corridor of grass leading to a classic sculpture is stunning, a well-framed view can also be created in modestly sized gardens. Trellises and gates surrounded with greenery can serve as a passageway for the eye. The appearance of garden ornaments can be enhanced with careful plantings around their contours.

A Secluded Spot

The most enjoyable English gardens are planned to furnish many little oases of privacy, where one can sit and reflect or meet a friend for a quiet chat. A garden, even a small one, should never entirely reveal itself in a single sweeping glance. Rather, it should unfold as a series of intimate vignettes: a bench or a table under a vine-covered arbor, rosebushes espaliered against the wall of a potting shed, even a reflecting pool shimmering on a terrace carved into a small slope.

Many gardeners construct a series of "rooms" in their gardens. Defined by tall evergreen hedges, trellises, fences, or other natural boundaries, these rooms can actually make a small garden seem larger as one strolls from one agreeable venue to another.

Take special care to create seating opportunities in your garden that offer a quiet haven for the visitor. Ideally these areas are not visible upon entering the garden but must be discovered as one meanders. Arbors and trellises can be particularly helpful in creating these private spaces.

THE GARDEN CONTAINER

Containers are a magnificent addition to a garden. They provide form and decoration, they furnish a suitable growing medium in places nature may have overlooked, and they allow plantings to decorate stairways and patios.

Most containers in English gardens are inspired by the classically detailed ornaments of Renaissance Italy. Nothing is more beautiful than a grouping of flowers or vines growing in weathered, lichen-covered urns embellished with sculpted garlands of fruit. Usually these are made of terra-cotta, stone, cement, or cast iron, although modern reproductions may be found in lightweight cast aluminum or faux stone. Wood, however, is also a much used material for garden containers. Particularly classic are the box-shaped planters decorated with finials that serve to highlight small trees.

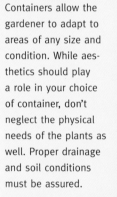

Containers allow the gardener to adapt to areas of any size and condition. While aesthetics should play a role in your choice of container, don't neglect the physical needs of the plants as well. Proper drainage and soil conditions must be assured.

THE CONSERVATORY

It is to the 18th-century architect and landscape designer Humphrey Repton that we owe the pleasure of sipping tea in the conservatory of an English house. Repton was a follower of the Picturesque movement, which advocated a relaxation of the strict symmetries that governed domestic decoration at that time. He also believed a sense of the garden could be brought inside, and thus designed conservatories that were attached to his clients' homes.

The addition of a conservatory resulted in a pleasant asymmetry to the architecture of a house and also brought the home owner into year-round contact with his or her beloved garden specimens. Conservatories remain extremely popular in England, not only for country houses but also for city town houses where budget and space permit.

For those who live in northern climates and are thus deprived of the opportunity for active year-round gardening, a conservatory is an excellent investment. To add one to your current home consider the many kits, spanning a range of budget levels, that are advertised through building and gardening magazines.

BRINGING IT INDOORS: BOUQUETS

That such gifted gardeners also exhibit an exquisite talent for creating floral bouquets should come as no surprise. After perfecting the soft and billowy style of their borders for so many generations, it is perhaps second nature for the English to bring these same qualities to their flower arrangements. But just as the "natural look" of the border is the result of careful planning and planting, the disarmingly relaxed look of the bouquet follows well-established guidelines.

A bouquet nearly always mixes two to four types of flowers. Exceptions might include grouping flowers of the same species that exhibit a variety of individual characteristics, such as multicolored pansies or a selection of antique roses.

Second, the flowers are not stripped of their greenery; the British firmly believe that the arrangement should echo the way flowers appear in nature.

Third, the overall effect of the arrangement should be loose and flowing, never dense and tightly bunched. To achieve this quintessentially English look, wispy flowers such as delphiniums are often introduced into the bouquet.

When it comes to color, most arrangements are quite soft and harmonious. One or two hues will play off the ever-present green of leaves and stems. A bouquet should never appear stiff or severe. Instead, it should capture a "just picked from the garden" feeling.

The most striking characteristic of the English bouquet is its soft, flowing quality. Whether a playful bunch of violets placed in a small ginger jar or an elegant array of peonies spilling from a celadon bowl, the arrangement is never contrived. With their depth of garden experience, the English hold an expansive view of natural beauty and do not limit themselves to perfectly formed blossoms. A holistic appreciation of leaves, stems, buds, and the many forms that flowers themselves may take underpins the manner in which they assemble a bouquet and gives rise to a limitless expression of their art.

THE KITCHEN

Like a steaming shepherd's pie or freshly baked scones smothered with jam and cream, the English kitchen warms the heart and soothes the soul. It is an ample, earthy room, filled with chunky pine furniture and a robust, enameled iron "cooker." There is no desire here for things sleek and modern. Rather, the kitchen is a place where tradition reigns and family members of all ages seek the timeless comforts of hearth and home.

Polly Devlin's kitchen exemplifies the English country style: natural materials abound, arrangements are informal, and there's space for the family to gather.

A Big, **Cozy** Place

A generous percentage of a home's square footage is cheerfully dedicated to the kitchen. Ideally the room is furnished not only with a table large enough to accommodate the family for informal meals, but also with a plump upholstered armchair or two, perhaps a small sofa. The kitchen serves as a cozy gathering place, an all-purpose room where friends can gossip over a cup of tea, children can do their homework or watch a bit of television, and the family's daily meals can be prepared and enjoyed.

Several characteristics combine to lend the kitchen its special warmth. Foremost is the abundance of wooden surfaces. Eschewing the high-tech synthetics that have become a staple of many modern kitchens, the English prefer the warmth and patina of wood for cabinets, countertops, and furniture. Pine, both painted and unpainted, is by far the most popular choice (see page 160). Complementing the wood are many other natural surfaces, such as stone used for fireplaces and floors, ceramic tile added as a backsplash, or rustic wicker baskets used to store fruits and vegetables.

Rich color is another important ele-

To create the feeling of an English country kitchen, borrow some ideas from Sue Hume. Create visual texture with herbs drying from ceiling racks and with family photographs and other objects. Include roomy upholstered seating where family members can relax.

ment in the kitchen. Here, as in other rooms of the house, the English do not hesitate to work with vibrant hues. Cabinets may be painted in Prussian blue or ivy green. Curtains dance with floral motifs featuring all manner of yellows, reds, and blues. Rugs may feature rich, earthy tones. And all the utilitarian necessities, such as jars, bowls, and cookware, cheer the room with their own rainbow of colors.

Finally, it is a lovably cluttered atmosphere that prevails. Dried herbs and copper pots hang from overhead racks. Earthenware crocks bursting with cooking utensils sit near the cooktop. A stack of magazines piles up near an easy chair. Open shelving displays eclectic collections of ceramic plates, teacups, and saucers. Ironstone bowls and pitchers gather on a sideboard, next to a trencher overflowing with fresh fruit.

The English kitchen, while upgraded in all its functional elements, manages to retain the appealing aesthetic qualities of its 18th- and 19th-century forerunners.

Although not a step to be taken lightly, the space to create a generously sized country kitchen can be borrowed from an adjacent room by taking down the common wall.

At the heart of every great English kitchen is a dazzling—and often eclectic—display of tablewares. Ideally the kitchen includes long open shelving or a hutch where these treasures can be displayed.

CHUNKY PINE

When thinking about English furniture, one might automatically call to mind mahogany as that nation's signature wood. In the kitchen, though, it is a softwood that reigns: pine. Often stripped and distressed with age, pine is used for tables, chairs, and cabinetry. Indeed, no other element is as essential to the look of a traditional English kitchen as its sturdy pine furniture.

Robust proportions and unpretentious design are key to the distinctive appearance of English pine furniture. Table legs, for example, are thick and sturdy. Squared off at the top, the legs are integrated into deep aprons, and decorated with only a few turnings. The legs of butcher-block tables are often unturned. Their chunky squared-off legs may feature only a small decorative groove at the height of a lower shelf, and then finish with just the slightest tapering at the foot. Cabinets typically are closed with simple raised-panel doors and accented with wooden or white ironstone knobs.

Favorite kitchen pieces made from pine include the dresser (often called a "hutch" in the United States), the sideboard, and plate racks made with long wooden dowels that allow plates to stand vertically. These freestanding units comprise what the English call an "unfitted" kitchen. The presence of individual pieces is strongly preferred over the sleekly homogenous appearance of modern "fitted" kitchens. (Wall cupboards are hung, but not permanently installed, in an unfitted kitchen.)

An unfitted kitchen need not rely on a supply of hard-to-find antique pieces. Many manufacturers are now creating a full range of unfitted furnishings that recall the charm of prewar English country kitchens. An even larger number, however, are offering fitted kitchens that evoke a period feel, but offer modern advantages of easier cleaning and greater storage capacity (see Resources). Plate racks, glazed cupboards, and cove molding are just three examples of the features designed into these installed units.

Whether you opt for an unfitted kitchen, a fitted kitchen, or a combination of the two, the use of pine is an indispensable element in creating an authentic English feeling in your kitchen.

OPPOSITE: Unfitted pine cupboards and plate racks confer an undeniably cozy look to the kitchen. And while delivering maximum charm, they also provide a highly efficient storage system. INSET: This center island butcher block has the perfect contours for a traditional English look: pleasingly robust and square. (See Resources.)

If a new, unfitted kitchen is not in the budget, consider modifying one or more of your existing cabinets to resemble an open-shelved cabinet. Simply remove the doors, hinges, and shelves. Add a back panel to cover the wall if necessary. Refit the shelves, adding a 1-by-1-inch wooden batten to the outside edge if the existing shelves are less than $3/4$-inch thick. Add molding to the new opening. Apply fresh paint or stain.

THE SAGA OF
THE AGA

Robust furnishings call for like-proportioned ovens and cooktops. Ironic as it may seem, the quintessentially English "cooker" was invented not by an Englishman but by a Swede: Dr. Gustav Dalen, the Nobel prize–winning physicist who created the original Aga cooker in the 1920s. Dr. Dalen's oven-and-cooktop has become wildly popular among the English; indeed, his success in Great Britain has eclipsed that in his native land.

Dalen's objective in designing the Aga was to create one highly efficient unit that would bake, boil, braise, grill, roast, steam, simmer, toast, and fry. The Aga works on the principle of stored heat, and so is never turned off. (For this reason,

too, the Aga is often the sole source of heat in the kitchen, obviating the need for a radiator.) The heat generated from a single combustion unit is accumulated in the ovens and hotplates, all made from massive iron castings.

Unlike the conventional range and oven, where one regulates the heat of the unit in use, each region of the Aga cooker holds a constant temperature. Depending on what one is preparing, the appropriate region will be used.

Highly efficient insulation prevents excessive heat loss. Thus, relatively little gas is needed to maintain the level of accumulated heat. The cooker also has the capacity to maintain a constant humidity, thereby preventing food from drying out and making exact timing less of a concern for many dishes.

KITCHEN
FLOORS

In keeping with the informal tone established by the pine furnishings, it is important that the kitchen floor look equally rustic. Whether or not a rug is laid over it, a natural flooring material, such as wood, stone, or terra-cotta tile, is key to achieving the right atmosphere. In the absence of synthetics elsewhere in the kitchen, a manmade flooring material would look out of place. Stone floors are particularly evocative of country manor houses; historically, they were prized for their ability to resist the fires that might be caused by an errant spark from a walk-in fireplace. Stone can be tiring to stand on, though, so make sure you do some test walking on stone before you make your final flooring choice.

Wood floors are an appropriate choice and offer many benefits; they are comfortable for cooks who may be spending extended periods on their feet, they are easy to sweep or vacuum, and, if desired, they can be decorated with paint. Wonderful country motifs such as checkerboards or stenciled flowers can easily be replicated by the do-it-yourselfer.

If you prefer a rug in your kitchen, choose one with a relaxed look. A kilim or a needlepoint rug placed under the table, or in a seating area, are perfect choices.

RIGHT: A wooden floor, softly worn through the years, is a beautiful complement to the painted cabinets. OPPOSITE: Durable kilims can stand up to heavy kitchen traffic.

THE PLEASURE
OF **TAKING TEA**

"I don't drink coffee, I take tea, my dear," sings the musician Sting in his 1987 hit "Englishman in New York," thereby offering in one succinct phrase absolute proof of his Englishness.

The English are indeed attached to their tea, and have spent centuries cultivating a lifestyle around it, replete with special foods and customs to accompany the sipping of the beloved brew. The era is long past, however, where all activity comes to a standstill at four o'clock so that tea may be taken. And the extending of an invitation to a formal tea party grows rarer with each passing year. Nevertheless, tea remains an integral part of English life, and a hostess will almost always offer tea with some cake or scones to an afternoon visitor.

One of the most delightful, albeit seasonal ways to enjoy tea with friends is to gather in the garden. The setting, while quite beautiful with its table dressed in printed cottons and laid with pretty porcelains, does not carry the imposing demands of a formal tea party indoors, and so is less intimidating to the uninitiated. Over the next six pages are suggestions for decorating a table, creating a menu, and, most important of all, brewing a delectable pot of tea.

Alison Gibbs's garden, in the heart of Kent, provides a sublimely beautiful setting for an afternoon tea. Note how well the wicker chairs work with the classic teak bench.

SETTING THE SCENE

A garden tea should reflect the freshness and splendor of the garden itself. Unless you have a beautiful wrought-iron or glass-topped garden table, use a tablecloth. A cotton or linen cloth printed with a floral motif is an excellent choice, although a plain, crisp white linen would also be appropriate. If your table is unattractive and you need to camouflage the base, place a ground-length skirt under the top cloth. Even if the base is quite presentable, you may still enjoy the hint of romance created when a table is draped in multiple layers. For our tea party shown at right, we selected a cloth with a stylized carnation motif in a soft coral hue and placed it over an under-skirt decorated with a small-scale ivy-green print.

Next, select china, flatware, and serving pieces that echo the tone of your table linens. These should be finer than every-day wares but not quite as formal as pieces used for a special dinner. China featuring a garden-related decoration, such as flowers, or the botanical motif we've used on our table, is a good choice. A mixture of cherished pieces collected at flea markets and antique shops would be a charming alternative. The serving bowls, plates, and trays can be of either porcelain or silver. Either of these would complement a silver tea service, if you have one. The center-piece, ideally, should come right from the garden.

THE MENU

Afternoon tea traditionally includes the three S's—a savory (usually in sandwich form), a scone, and a sweet. The menu opens with dainty tea sandwiches. Without exception, these are made on thinly sliced, finely textured bread from which the crust has been removed. At our tea, pictured at right, the bread has been buttered (real butter, please!) and then layered with paper-thin slices of cucumber that have been very lightly salted. (We left the skin on the cucumber to add a bit of color to the sandwich, but some people prefer it peeled.) The sandwiches are then cut into small pieces—quarters, triangles, or rounds—and arranged attractively on a platter garnished with a few sprigs of parsley.

The next course on the menu features freshly baked scones (see recipe page 170) served with jam and whipped (or clotted) cream. We also offer Scottish pancakes made from a slightly sweetened batter turned into silver dollar–sized crêpes. Some hostesses will also offer a tea bread.

We followed our scones with an almond cake and a rhubarb tansy, a sweet pudding made from rhubarb harvested at the peak of the season (see recipe page 171).

Tea is poured or replenished with each course. It is most polite to offer a selection of teas. To accompany the tea, set out milk, slices of lemon, and cubes of sugar. Cream is never served with tea.

INSET: For our center-piece, we gathered sweet peas in a range of hues and clustered them in a porcelain vase.

TOP LEFT: Appropriate fillings for tea sandwiches include cucumber, smoked salmon, egg salad, thin slices of ham or turkey, fresh tomato, and watercress. TOP RIGHT: In addition to the classic scones, our hostess included Scottish pancakes. It is appropriate to serve both on the same plate accompanied by jam and whipped cream. BOTTOM LEFT: Many types of cakes, tarts, and cookies can be served for a garden tea. Avoid frozen desserts, however, or anything that might melt or curdle in the sun. BOTTOM RIGHT: A garden tea provides the perfect opportunity to mix pretty crystal pieces with your favorite porcelains. Don't hesitate to use a combination of different services.

MAKING A PERFECT SCONE

Alison Gibbs, who lives in Kent, graciously allowed us to photograph the step-by-steps of making a proper scone (correctly pronounced, she says, as "skawn"). Alison claims it is far easier to make a scone than many realize; the secret is in the consistency of the batter. "You don't want the mixture too dry," she says. "It should feel a bit sticky to the fingers."

1. Preheat the oven to 350°F. Assemble your ingredients: 2 cups of flour, 1 level teaspoon baking powder, 3 tablespoons softened butter, ¼ cup sugar, 1 egg, and ½ cup milk, plus a couple of tablespoons to brush the tops of the scones before baking.

Sieve the flour and baking powder together into a large bowl. Cut in the butter with a pastry blender until the mixture resembles fine crumbs. Stir in the sugar. Whisk the egg and ½ cup milk together in a separate bowl, then stir into the flour mixture to form a soft, somewhat sticky, dough. Do not overstir.

2. Turn the dough out onto a floured board. Being careful not to overwork the dough, pat it flat with the palms of the

hands to a thickness of about ¾ inch. With a cookie cutter or glass, cut the dough into two-inch rounds. Place the rounds onto a greased or Teflon-coated cookie sheet or baking pan. Alison uses a synthetic sheet liner, available through kitchen supply catalogs, that prevents the scones from sticking to the pan and allows them to cook evenly.

3. Using the remaining milk, brush a small amount of milk onto the top of each scone. This will help bring a golden finish to the scone when it is baked.

4. Bake the scones for 10 minutes, or until golden brown. Remove from the oven, allow them to cool slightly, then serve with strawberry jam (or other jam of your choice) and whipped heavy cream.

MAKING A RHUBARB TANSY

When the garden reaches its peak production of sweet red rhubarb, it's the perfect time to make rhubarb tansy—a dessert favorite that harks back to Elizabethan days. (The word "tansy" simply refers to a fruit pudding.) This recipe was handed down to Alison Gibbs by Granny Galbraith, her maternal grandmother in Scotland.

1. Use a heavy pot, such as the enameled cast-iron type manufactured by Le Creuset. Assemble your ingredients: 1 pound rhubarb cut into 1½-inch pieces, ¼ pound butter cut into 1-inch pieces, 1 cup sugar, 2 egg yolks, ½ cup heavy cream, and the juice of 1 lemon.

2. Put the rhubarb and butter into the pot and place over medium heat. As the butter melts, gradually stir in the sugar. Continue to cook until the rhubarb becomes tender, about 5 minutes. Remove from heat and allow to cool slightly so that the eggs, when added,

will not cook to the point of scrambling. Whisk together the egg yolks and cream and stir into rhubarb mixture. Reduce the heat to low and return the pot to the stove. Heat slowly, stirring continuously until the mixture thickens, about 4 to 5 minutes. Do not allow the mixture to boil. Stir in the lemon juice and remove from the heat.

3. When the tansy has cooled to room temperature, place it in the refrigerator for a few minutes. It should be served just slightly chilled. (If you've made it ahead of time, allow it to warm up to just below room temperature.) Serve in pretty dessert dishes and garnish with a few fresh mint leaves and a light sprinkling of sugar.

BREWING TEA

Passionate tea drinkers abound with theories about the "right way" to brew the "perfect" cup. Many tell you to run water from the tap for a period of time (to release impurities or to properly aerate); others caution against "underboiling" or "overboiling" the water. Such debates can be needlessly intimidating. The truth is that a satisfying cup of tea can be brewed by observing a few guidelines.

1. Start with a good-quality tea. Go to a shop that sells specialty teas and sample the fragrance of several. Let your olfactory senses be your guide. Good tea smells—well—good! The fullest, richest flavor will be achieved by using leaf tea, but when time is limited, a tea bag is perfectly serviceable. (Tea bags typically contain the pulverized residue or small fragments of tea leaves; they do not deliver as much flavor as the whole leaf.)

2. Use good-tasting water. If your tap water is hard or tastes of chlorine, use bottled water instead.

3. Prewarm your teapot. Fill the pot with very hot or boiling water and swirl it around until the porcelain or earthenware feels warm. Then discard the water. Prewarming will ensure that the tea you are brewing doesn't give up its heat to a cold container.

4. Measure loose tea into the pot; you will need 1 teaspoonful for each cup you are brewing—plus "1 for the pot," if you like it strong. Some people prefer to enclose the tea in a mesh ball, others prefer to strain the tea. Let the tea steep for between 3 and 5 minutes, according to the directions on the tin of tea, or to taste. (Whole-leaf tea generally takes a bit longer to steep than bagged tea.)

5. When serving tea, always prepare a second pot filled with water that has been brought to a boil. Those who prefer a more diluted tea can add a bit of warm water to their cup.

6. According to your taste, add sugar, lemon, or milk (never cream, which is too thick) to your tea. (Many English pour milk in their cup first, before the tea. This ritual follows the same theory, in reverse, as heating the pot. Tradition has it that the milk protects fine porcelain from possible cracking.)

THE FRESH TASTE OF LEMON CRUSH

Summertime in England calls forth a rainbow of cool, refreshing drinks called "crushes"
that are made with fruits and berries. One of the most popular is elderflower crush, made from
the small white blossoms that grow on elderflower bushes alongside many country lanes. Since
elderflower is not universally available, we've prepared a popular alternative, lemon crush.
The basic ingredients are plentiful and the taste is sublime!

1. To make Lemon Crush for four, you will need to assemble 4 lemons, 1 cup sugar, and cold water to dilute to taste.

2. Wash the lemons, but do not peel them. Cut into quarters.

3. Place lemon quarters in a food processor and pulse until they are reduced to a very coarse purée. Add the sugar and pulse once

or twice to blend. Transfer the purée to a pitcher. Add cold water to taste—we added about 16 ounces.

4. Allow to stand for a few minutes so that the coarse bits will sink to the bottom of the pitcher.

5. Serve over ice in old-fashioned glasses and garnish with edible flowers or mint leaves.

IDEA NOTEBOOK

In assembling the furniture for an unfitted kitchen, **A FOCAL POINT SHOULD BE THE HUTCH.** Select proportions as ample as your space allows to create a traditional atmosphere. (See Resources.)

To enhance the comfort of pine chairs and add a touch of charm, don't forget **COTTON-COVERED SEAT CUSHIONS.**

Note how effective the **DEEP PORCELAIN SINK** is at creating a rustic tone in this kitchen. The **PINE PANEL ON THE DISHWASHER** front works exceptionally well in this scheme. (See Resources.)

Don't forget to **USE OVERHEAD SPACE** to store and display cookware, baskets, herbs, and so on. If you don't have exposed beams, consider installing pot racks. (See Resources.)

Center island **BUTCHER-BLOCK TABLES** are both practical and beautiful, adding quality work space as well as storage to the kitchen. Look for **LOVABLY CHUNKY LINES.** (See Resources.)

The amount of available wall space in your kitchen will dictate the overall size of the **PLATE RACK** you can install. The variations on moldings, trims, and configurations are endless— **SELECT WHATEVER PLEASES YOUR EYE.** (See Resources.)

HOW TO SPEAK ENGLISH

"Isn't that in good nick," I heard a smartly dressed English woman say, gesturing toward a table in a London antique shop. "Good nick?" I said to myself, "I wonder what *that* means?" Before the week was out, my American-English vocabulary had failed to elucidate two additional usages of the word "nick": a teenager complaining that a school chum had "nicked" her boyfriend, and a poster explaining how the police would without fail "nick" a shoplifter if caught in the act.[1]

Like most Americans, I was well aware of the clichés about England and the United States being divided by a common language. I knew the British refer to a "truck" as a "lorry," that the "mail" is called the "post," and that, had I grown up in England rather than in one of her former colonies, my "mom" would be known as my "mum." Beyond the amusing differences of a few terms, however, I had always believed British English and American English to be identical languages.

I have been disabused of this notion! After spending some time in England, I now understand that the chasm between the two languages is considerable, reaching far beyond a few conflicting appellations. In fact, you could say the so-called divide extends to the very foundations of verbal expression. From the standpoint of vocabulary alone, I learned that linguists have identified some four thousand words having different meanings in British and American English. But it is the differences, both subtle and overt, in the way we actually structure our speech that fascinate me more.

Take the use of adverbs, for example. When we, as Americans, want to stress the power of an adjective, as in "a boring lesson," we often simply add the word "very"—making it a *very* boring lesson. But British speakers typically take a more colorful approach. A noun, such as "monument," is frequently converted into an adverb, making the whole affair *monumentally* boring.

But the key to British English does not lie in the use of dazzling modifiers. Paradoxically, colorful descriptors are generally reserved to bring life to otherwise ho-hum affairs. When witnessing a truly spectacular event, the speaker often understates the action. For example, a sports broadcaster reports on a horrific collision of runners as the leader trips over a hurdle. Half the field goes down, and the greatest upset of the year unfolds before his eyes. The commentary? "Bit of mismeasurement there."

Indirectness, in fact, is critical to speaking British English. Indeed, proper society would crumble without the ability *not* to say what one means. When blatantly disagreeing, for example, direct confrontation is to be avoided at all costs. Instead of informing your interlocutor that you believe him or her to be sadly off the point, you murmur a vague "I wonder . . ." or "I dare say. . . ." When pressed for an actual opinion, one is allowed the demure "Well, I really wouldn't like to say."

And finally, a bit of general advice for the speaker of American English striving for fluency in British English: concentrate less on vocabulary and more on nuance. Even a *monolithically* vast lexicon won't compensate for an inability to snatch ambiguity from the jaws of precision.

[1]The meaning of "nick" in these three situations, in the order of appearance, is (1) condition, (2) to steal, and (3) to apprehend.

RESOURCES

A rich array of English products for the home is available throughout the United States. Large department stores such as Bloomingdale's, Neiman-Marcus, Bergdorf-Goodman, and Saks Fifth Avenue are good resources, as are the many specialty home furnishings stores found in most large cities. If you are shopping in England, a similar array of products will be found in Harrods, Harvey Nichols, Liberty of London, or Peter Jones. Additionally, the public is welcome in the Chelsea Harbour Interior Design Center in the southwest section of London. It is an easy cab ride from downtown and most of the prominent manufacturers maintain showrooms there.

Below is a list of retailers in the United States who carry many of the items shown in this book. Telephone and fax numbers of the companies in England are also provided, should you wish to contact a company directly. (Note: When calling or faxing England from the United States, you must dial 011-44. When calling long-distance within England, you must add a 0 before the number listed.)

PRODUCT INFORMATION

Room to Relax

England is an antiques hunter's paradise. From London to Liverpool, one can find treasures of all sorts. I had the pleasure of meeting Maddy Kingzett, an American woman who married an Englishman, settled in London, and started her own antiques business. The art and objects shown on pages 92, 93, 94, and 102 are part of her collection. Ms. Kingzett has many similar pieces available for sale and is happy to work with clients searching for particular types of objects. She can be reached in London.

Maddy Kingzett Antiques
68 Camberwell Grove
SE5 8RF London
171-701-7551

Children
Page 107: girl's smock dress: Mini Boden
Page 112: boy's short set: Mini Boden

FABRIC

Bennison
(Shown on page 22.)
16 Holbein Place
London SW1 8NL
171-730-8076

76 Greene Street
New York, NY 10012
212-941-1212
212-941-5587 (fax)

George Spencer
4 West Halkin Street
London SW1
171-235-1501
171-235-1502 (fax)

Laura Ashley Limited
(Shown on pages 2, 8, 73, 74.)
27 Bagleys Lane
London SW6 2AR
171-736-6700
171-731-8530 (fax)
For retail locations in the United States, call 800-429-7678.

Liberty of London Prints Ltd.
(Shown on pages 6, 72, 73, 82, 139.)
313 Merton Road
London SW18 5JS
181-870-7631
181-871-3175 (fax)

For retail locations in the United States, call:

Osborne & Little/Liberty of London
979 Third Avenue, Suite 520
New York, NY 10022
212-751-3333
212-752-6027 (fax)

49 Temperley Road
London SW12 8QE
181-675-2255
181-673-8254 (fax)

90 Commerce Road
Stamford, CT 06902
203-359-1500
203-353-0854 (fax)

Mulberry
Kilver Court
Shepton Mallet
Somerset BA4 5NF
1749-340-500
1761-233-519 (fax)
Mulberry home furnishings is represented in the United States by Lee Jofa. For retail locations in the United States, call 800-4-Lee Jofa (800-453-3563).

G.P.& J. Baker
For retail locations call 1-800-4-Lee Jofa (800-453-3563).

Lee Jofa
For retail locations call 1-800-4-Lee Jofa (800-453-3563).

Monkwell
For retail locations call 1-800-4-Lee Jofa (800-453-3563).

Nina Campbell
(Shown on page 38.)
9 Walton Street
SW3 2JD London
171-225-1011
171-225-0644 (fax)

Ramm, Son & Crocker Limited
(Shown on pages 74, 75.)
Chelsea Harbour Design Center
Chelsea Harbour
London SW10 0XE
171-352-0931
171-352-0935 (fax)
For showroom locations in the United States, call:

55 Cabot Boulevard
Mansfield, MA 02078
800-756-7266
800-332-8256 (fax)

TABLE/BED LINENS

Laura Ashley
See previous listing.

Nina Campbell
See previous listing.

Ralph Lauren Home Collection
1185 Avenue of the Americas
New York, NY 10020
For retail information, call
212-642-8700.

The White House
40-41 Conduit Street
London W1R 9FB
For mail order sales contact:
171-629-3521
171-629-8269 (fax)

WALLPAPER

Mulberry
See previous listing.

Nina Campbell
See previous listing.

Osborne & Little
See previous listing.

Ramm, Son & Crocker Limited
See previous listing.

Sanderson
112-120 Brompton Road
London SW3
171-584-3344
For retail information in the United States, call 212-319-7220.

UPHOLSTERED FURNITURE

Laura Ashley
See previous listing.

Lee Jofa
See previous listing.

Mulberry
For retail locations call 1-800-4-Lee Jofa.

Ralph Lauren Home Collection
See previous listing.

Ramm, Son & Crocker Limited
See previous listing.

PORCELAIN AND CERAMICS

Asprey
Trump Tower
725 Fifth Avenue
New York, NY 10022
For other locations in the United States, call 800-883-2777. In New York City, call 212-688-1811 or fax 212-688-2749.

Nina Campbell
by Rosenthal
For retail information call 201-804-8000, x221.

Spode
1265 Glen Avenue
Moorestown, NJ 08057
For retail information call 800-257-7189.

Royal Doulton
For retail information call 908-356-7880.

Ralph Lauren Home Collection
See previous listing.

Wedgwood

Wedgwood is sold through fine retailers nationwide. For information call 732-938-5800. In select locations you can find a Wedgwood Store. For locations call 800-677-7860.

CRYSTAL

Asprey
See previous listing.

Ralph Lauren Home Collection
See previous listing.

Stuart & Sons Ltd.
Redhouse Glassworks
Stourbridge, West Midlands DY8 4AA
1384–828-282
1384–704-63 (fax)

SILVER

Asprey
See previous listing.

James Robinson
480 Park Avenue
New York, NY 10022
212-752-6166

S.J. Shrubsole
104 East 57 Street
New York, NY 10022
212-753-8920

BATH FURNISHINGS

Czech & Speak
244-254 Cambridge Heath Road
London E2 9DA
For distributors in the United States, call 181-980-4567 or fax 181-981-7232.

KITCHEN FURNISHINGS/COOKERS

Aga
P.O. Box 30
Ketley Telford
Shropshire TF1 1BR
1952-642000
1952-243138 (fax)
Aga cookers are available through more than 75 distributors in the United States. A partial directory follows. If your city does not appear, contact the company in England for a complete list.

Aga Cookers West
San Francisco, California
415-822-0183

Thurston Kitchens
Boulder, Colorado
303-449-4001

Bartenfeld's
Roswell, Georgia
770-587-2800

Kitchen Classics
Willmette, Illinois
847-251-9540

Bonnie Fleming, LLC
Charlotte, North Carolina
704-338-9245

Showcase Appliance Center
Santa Fe, New Mexico
505-982-5563

Legendary English Cookers
Fairport, New York
716-223-4417

Coulter Kitchens & Interior
Akron, Ohio
216-434-6666

Haydn Cutler Co.
Fort Worth, Texas
817-336-2425

Sutter Home & Hearth
Woodinville, Washington
206-486-9286

Chalon UK Limited, Hambridge Mill
(Shown on pages 160, 161, 175.)
Hambridge Somerset
TA10 0BP England
1458-252-374
1458-251-192 (fax)
Chalon is available through the following United States distributors: in North Carolina, South Carolina, Georgia, Alabama, Mississippi, Tennessee, Florida, and Colorado:

Oliver Walker
Atlanta, Georgia
404-262-1408
404-262-9862 (fax)

Fort Lauderdale, Florida
954-929-0031

Denver, Colorado
303-744-1404

In California, Arizona, Nevada, Texas, Oklahoma, and Louisiana:

Guy Chaddock
San Francisco, California
415-621-8828

Los Angeles, California
310-271-3650

Dallas, Texas
214-744-9124

In Washington, Oregon, Montana, and Utah:

Michael Folks
Seattle, Washington
206-762-6776

Smallbone Devize
(Shown on page 174.)
105-109 Fulham Road
London SW3 6RL
171-589-5998

In the United States, Smallbone Devize is available through:

de Giulio kitchen design inc.
1121 Central Avenue
Wilmette, IL 60091
847-256-8833
847-256-8842 (fax)

John Lewis of Hungerford
278-306 Oxford Street
London W1A 1EX
171-629-7711
171-629-0849 (fax)

GARDEN TOOLS

The English Garden Collection
P.O. Box 1030
Langley/Slough
Berkshire SL3 8BX
Catalog requests from within the UK, call 0800-103-000, and from the United States, 1753-588-413, or fax 1753-730-067.

Smith & Hawkens
Call 800-776-3336 for a catalog.

GARDEN FURNISHINGS

Haddonstone Ltd.
The Forge House
East Haddon
Northhampton NN6 8DB
1604-770711
1604-770027 (fax)

Haddonstone USA Ltd
201 Heller Place, Interstate Business Park
Bellmawr, NJ 08031
609-931-7011
609-931-0040 (fax)
email: sales@haddonstone.com

Smith & Hawkins
See previous listing.

Gardeners Eden
Call 800-822-9600 for a catalog.

GARDEN TOURS

Greenfingers Garden Tours
Upper Kennards
Leigh
Kent TN11 8RE
1732-832-160 (tel/fax)

The National Garden Scheme
Many private gardens in England can be toured. The National Garden Scheme publishes an annual guide called The Yellow Book that lists all private gardens open for touring. The Yellow Book can be purchased in the United States through the British Rail bookstore. Additionally, the bookstore sells guides to historic homes and other points of interest. For information, call 212-490-6688 or fax 212-490-0219.

Sissinghurst Garden
To visit this legendary garden of Vita Sackville-West located in the county of Kent, call 1580-712-850 or 1580-715-330, or fax 1580-713-911 (all numbers in England).

CLASSIC CHILDREN'S CLOTHING

Mini Boden
Midland Terrace
Victoria Road
London NW10 6DB
181-453-1535
181-453-1445 (fax)

The White House
40-41 Conduit Street
London W1R 9FB
171-629-3521
171-629-8269 (fax)

INTERIOR DECORATORS

Nina Campbell
(Shown on pages 39, 62.)
9 Walton Street
London SW3 25D
171-225-1011
171-225-0644 (fax)

George Cooper
(Shown on pages 11, 25, 51, 62, 86, 87, 88, 90, 97, 98, 121.)
Hinton House
Ablington/Cirencester
Gloucestershire GL7 5NY
1285-740-233
1285-740-282 (fax)

Christophe Gollut
(Shown on pages 14, 42, 96.)

Virginia Howard
(Shown on pages 44, 51, 99.)
116 Fulham Road
SW3 6HU London
171-370-4101
171-370-4123 (fax)

Anne-Louise Little
(Shown on pages 25, 52, 98.)
24 Fabian Road
SW6 7TZ
171-385-0962
171-381-5931 (fax)

Alidad Mahloudji
(Shown on pages 15, 51, 56, 60, 120.)
34 Ives Street
SW3 London
171-581-4991
171-581-3286 (fax)

Sally Metcalfe
(Shown on pages 5, 13, 17, 18, 30, 49, 57, 121.)

Sally Metcalfe can be contacted at:
George Spencer Designs
4 West Halkin Street
SW1X 8JA
171-235-1501
171-235-1502 (fax)

PLACES OF INTEREST/TRADITIONAL ENGLISH INNS

Llangoed Hall
(Shown on pages 2, 8, 19, 147, 148.)
Llyswen, Brecon
Powys
Wales LD3 0YP
1874-754-525
1874-754-545 (fax)

Keswick Hall
701 Country Club Drive
Keswick, VA 22947
800-Ashley-1
804-977-4171 (fax)

The Inn at Perry Cabin
308 Watkins Lane
St. Michaels, MD 21663
800-722-2949
410-745-3348 (fax)

The National Trust
The National Trust is dedicated to preserving historic properties throughout England. Many of these properties are available for holiday rentals. For information, contact the United State affiliate of The National Trust, the Royal Oak Foundation:

Royal Oak Foundation
800-913-6565
In New York City call
212-966-6565.
web site: http://www.royal-oak.org
email: general@royal-oak.org

Touring in Great Britain
For information on travel planning in England and elsewhere in the U.K., call:

The British Tourist Authority
551 Fifth Avenue
Suite 701
New York, NY 10176
800-GO2-BRITAIN 462-2748
212-986-2200 (New York City only)
212-986-1188 (fax)
web site:
http://www.visitbritain.com

SUGGESTED READING

Atterbury, Paul., ed., *A.W.N. Pugin, Master of the Gothic Revival.* New Haven, Conn.: Yale University Press, 1995.

Calloway, Stephen, and Stephen Jones. *Traditional Style.* London: Mitchell Beazley, 1994.

Gore, Alan and Ann. *The History of English Interiors.* London: Phaidon Press, 1991.

Miller, Judith. *Judith Miller's Guide to Period-Style Curtains & Soft Furnishings.* Woodstock, N.Y.: The Overlook Press, 1996.

Naylor, Gillian, ed. *William Morris by Himself.* Boston, Mass.: Little, Brown and Company, 1996.

Parissien, Steven. *Adam Style.* London: Phaidon Press, 1992.

————. *The Georgian House.* London: Aurum Press, 1995.

————. *Palladian Style.* London: Phaidon Press, 1994.

————. *Regency Style.* London: Phaidon Press, 1992.

Thornton, Peter. *Authentic Decor.* New York/Avenel, N.J.: Crescent Books, 1993.

Watkin, David. *English Architecture.* London: Thames and Hudson, Ltd., 1979.

Wrey, Caroline. *The Complete Book of Curtains and Drapes.* Woodstock, N.Y.: The Overlook Press, 1991.

INDEX

Page numbers in *italic* refer to captions.

Adam, Robert, 19–21, 49, 55,
      79
Adam style, 79, 138
Aesthetic style, 72, 139
Aga cookers, 163
Alidad, 15, 50, 61, 127
animals
      dogs, 26, 32
      motifs, 23, 52
      portraits, 26
architecture, 29, 78, 81
Art Nouveau style, 72
Arts and Crafts movement, 50,
      72, 82, 139
artworks
      animals in, 26
      botanical prints, 25
      hanging, 30, 48, 52
      portraits, 71
Asian influences, 21, 26, 72, 74

Banqueting House, 78
Barrie, James M., 106
Barton, Lilly, 106
Barton, Ned, 108
bathrooms, 101–2
bedrooms, 84–87, 104–5
      furniture, 84, 87–90, 92
      gathered fabrics, 91
      nurseries, 106, 110
      room to relax in, 92
      walls, 98–101
      window treatments, 97–98
beds, 84, 87–90
      four-poster canopy, 88–89
      upholstered headboards, 89
bed skirts (valences), 88, 89
Berger, Diane, 25, 35, 47, 52,
      102, 127
botanical prints, 25
Brideshead Revisited (Waugh), 32,
      106

cabinets, kitchen, 155, 156, 160
Calloway, Stephen, 47
Campbell, Nina, 38, 62
candlesticks, 123
carpets, 55–59
centerpieces, 132, 168
chairs
      Chippendale, 80, 133
      dining, 121, 133, 134
children
      nurseries, 106, 110
      tea, 110
      toys, 106, 113
china, 130
chintzes, 74, 75
Chippendale, Thomas, 19–21, 52,
      74, 80, 133
Classical period, 138
Colefax & Fowler, 83
collectibles, 16, 66–68
color schemes, 16, 29, 49, 73, 75
      in bedrooms, 98, 101
      in dining rooms, 117
      in kitchens, 155–56
comfort, 7–10, 42, 87
conservatories, 149
Cooper, George, 25, 50, 62, 87
coronas, 89
crystal, 131

Dalen, Gustav, 163
Devlin, Polly, 12, 32, 41, 52,
      152
dining rooms, 114–18, 134–35
      centerpieces, 132
      furniture, 118–21, 133
      sterling silver, 123–24
      tables, 118–21, 133
      table settings, 127–31
      walls, 117
dinner services, 130
dogs, 26, 32
draperies, 61–62, 64, 97
drawing rooms, 38–41, 76–77
      floors, 55–59

furniture, 41–44, 76
walls, 47–50
windows, 61–65

earthenware, 130
eccentricity, 32–36
Elizabethan period, 137
Elizabeth I, Queen, 50
Elliott, Harry, 108
English language, differences between
      U.S. and British, 176

fabrics
      Arts and Crafts, 72, 82
      Asian-inspired, 74
      chintzes, 74, 75
      floral motifs, 23–26, 73
      gathered, 91
      gently faded, 73
      Old England, 73
      tailored, 74–75
      toile de Jouy, 88–89
      on walls, 50, 98
      for window treatments, 61–62,
            64, 97
floors
      carpets and rugs, 15, 55–59, 164
      in drawing rooms, 55–59
      in kitchens, 164
      rush matting, 58
floral motifs, 23–26, 49–50, 58,
      73, 74
flowers
      bouquets, 77, 150–51
      centerpieces, 132, 168
Fowler, John, 49, 83
furniture, 10, 12, 16
      in bedrooms, 84, 87–90, 92
      in dining rooms, 118–21, 133
      in drawing rooms, 41–44, 76
      in kitchens, 155, 160, 174, 175
      lacquered, 21
      upholstered, 9, 30
      wood, 19–21, 88

gardens, 140–44
    beds and borders, 145
    containers, 148
    fencing, 143
    framing views in, 146
    hedges, 143, *143*
    lawn, 144
    outdoor rooms, 41, *147*
    seating, 147
    tea in, 167–68
Garnet, Andy, 140
Georgian period, 19, 21, 84, 133, 138
Gibb, Alison, *167*, 170, 171
glassware, 131
Gollut, Christophe, 15, 42
Goodhew, Ann, *110*
Goodhew, Victoria, *110*
Gore, Alan, 75, 117
Gore, Ann, 117
Gothic period, 137
Gothic Revival style, 50, 81
graphic patterns, 29–30, 52

half-testers, 89
hedges, 143, *143*
Henry III, King, 49–50
Henry VIII, King, 50
Hepplewhite, George, 133
Hobhouse, Penelope, 143
Hopkins, Anthony, 114
Howard, Virginia, *44*, 50
Hume, Sue, 64, *155*

India, 75
Ishiguro, Kazuo, 114

Jacobean period, 137
Jones, Inigo, 47, 78
Jones, Stephen, 47

Kilpatrick, Andrew, 114
Kilpatrick, Helen, 114
Kingzett, Emily, *110*
Kingzett, Maddy, 92
Kingzett, Veronica, *110*
kitchens, 152–56, 174–75
    cabinets, 155, 156, 160
    floors, 164

furniture, 155, 160, *174*, *175*
    stoves, 163
    unfitted, 160, *174*
Knox, Christine, *117*

Lancaster, Nancy, 49, 83
language, differences between U.S. and
        British English, 176
lemon crush, 173
Liberty & Co., 72, 82
linens
    bed, 88–89
    table, *128*, 129, 168
Little, Ann-Louise, 25, 52
living rooms. *See* drawing rooms
London, 29
Long Barn, 140, 143

Mackintosh, Charles Rennie, 72
Magan, Maxime, 140, *143*, 144
Mahloudji, Alidad, 15, *50*, 61, 127
mahogany, 19–21, 88, 118
Maugham, Syrie, 21
Metcalfe, Sally, *4*, 12
Morris, William, 26, 58, 72, 82

napkins, 128, 129
nature motifs, 23–26, 72, 74, 98
neoclassical period, 64, 78
nurseries, 106, *110*

Orient. *See* Asian influences
Oriental carpets, 55, *57*

Palladian period, 138
Parissien, Steven, 131
pattern, 12
    Arts and Crafts, 72, 82
    in carpets, 58
    floral motifs, 23–26, 49–50, 58,
        73, 74
    graphic, 29–30, 52
pelmets, 61, 62–64, 97–98
period styles, 136–39
    window treatments, 64
Peter Pan (Barrie), 106
pictures. *See* artworks

pine, 155, 160
placemats, 128, 129
porcelain, 130
Post, Peggy, *16*
pottery, 130
print rooms, 52
Pugin, A. W. N., 81

Queen Anne period, 19
Queen's House, Greenwich, 47, 78

recipes
    lemon crush, 173
    rhubarb tansy, 171
    scones, 170
Regency period, 64, 133, 138
Regency stripe, 75
Remains of the Day (Ishiguro), 114
Repton, Humphrey, 149
rhubarb tansy, 171
Rossetti, Dante Gabriel, 82
rugs, 15, 55–59, 164
rush matting, 58
Ruskin, John, 72, 82

Sackville-West, Vita, *140*
St. Michael's House, *143*
sandwiches, tea, 168, *169*
scones, 168, 170
shades, fabric, 65
Sheffield plate, 124
Sheraton, Thomas, 19–21, 133
silver, sterling, 123–24
sofas, 42
stoves, Aga, 163

tablecloths, 129
table mats, *127*, 129
tables, dining, 118–21, 133
table settings, 127–31, 168
tansy, rhubarb, 171
tea, 167–68
    brewing, 172
    children's, *110*
    menu, 168, *169*
    recipes, 170, 171, 173
    sandwiches, 168, *169*
    serving, 168, 172

tea caddies, 123
textiles, 10, 12
    See also fabrics; rugs
toile de Jouy, 88–89
toys, 106, 113
Tudor period, 137

unfitted kitchens, 160, 174
Upper Kennards, 143

valances. *See* pelmets
valences (bed skirts), 88, 89
Victorian period, 49, 64, 139

visually charged atmosphere,
    12–16
vocabulary, British, 176

walls
    in bedrooms, 98–101
    in dining rooms, 117
    in drawing rooms, 47–50
    hanging artworks, 30, 48, 52
    moldings, 47, 48, 117
    upholstering, 50, 98
    wallpaper, 49–50, 101
    wood paneling, 50
Waugh, Evelyn, 32, 106
Wendy houses, 106, 110

Whistler, James McNeill, 26
Wilde, Oscar, 32, 72
Wilton House, 78
window treatments, 30
    in bedrooms, 97–98
    draperies, 61–62, 64, 97
    in drawing rooms, 61–65
    pelmets, 61, 62–64, 97–98
    shades, 65
    tiebacks, 65
Windsor Castle, 81
wood, 19–21, 88
    in kitchens, 155, 160
    paneling, 50
Wright, Frank Lloyd, 72